Ghosting the News
Local Journalism and the Crisis of American Democracy

COLUMBIA GLOBAL REPORTS
NEW YORK

Ghosting the News
Local Journalism and the Crisis of American Democracy

Margaret Sullivan

Canada

United
States

Brazil

Ghosting the News:
Local Journalism and the Crisis of American Democracy
Copyright © 2020 by Margaret Sullivan
All rights reserved

Published by Columbia Global Reports
91 Claremont Avenue, Suite 515
New York, NY 10027
globalreports.columbia.edu
facebook.com/columbiaglobalreports
@columbiaGR

Library of Congress Cataloging-in-Publication Data
Names: Sullivan, Margaret, 1957- author.
Title: Ghosting the News: Local Journalism and the Crisis of American Democracy /
    Margaret Sullivan.
Description: New York: Columbia Global Reports, 2020. |
    Includes bibliographical references. |
Identifiers: LCCN 2020009379 | ISBN 9781733623780 (paperback)
Subjects: LCSH: Journalism, Regional--Political aspects--United States. | Local mass
    media--United States. | Press and politics--United States--History--21st century.
Classification: LCC PN4784.L6 S85 2020 | DDC 071/.3--dc23
LC record available at https://lccn.loc.gov/2020009379

Book design by Strick&Williams
Map design by Jeffrey L. Ward
Author photograph by Michael Benabib

Printed in the United States of America

For Alex and Grace, and for journalists everywhere

CONTENTS

Ghosting the News

Local Journalism and
the Crisis of American
Democracy

Introduction

Barbara O'Brien's article was routine-enough fare for a local newspaper. It would not go on to win a journalism award or change the world. It didn't even make Sunday's front page on that day in May of 2019. It merely was the kind of day-in-and-day-out local reporting that makes secretive town officials unhappy because of what they can't get away with, and lets local taxpayers know how their money is being spent.

O'Brien, who reports on several suburban towns for the *Buffalo News*, had found that the Orchard Park police chief, who was retiring abruptly, would receive an unexplained $100,000 as part of his departure. A few weeks before O'Brien's story was published, she had asked town officials for the chief's separation agreement, but they said it couldn't be released because it included a confidentiality clause. Why would there be such a thing, she asked. The town supervisor referred the questions to the town attorney, who wouldn't comment.

O'Brien doggedly took the next steps, as her story explained:

14   *The Buffalo News* obtained a copy of the sixteen-page agree-
       ment after filing a Freedom of Information Law request with
       the town. Keeping such a contract private is in violation of
       the Freedom of Information Law, according to Robert J.
       Freeman, executive director of the state Committee on Open
       Government.

       "The contract is public, notwithstanding a confidentiality
       clause," Freeman said. "The courts have held time and again
       that an agreement requiring confidentiality cannot overcome
       rights conferred in the Freedom of Information Law."

Examining the agreement, O'Brien came across the $100,000
payout, and wrote the story. And she would, of course, keep
digging—because that is what diligent local reporters do. But
there are fewer and fewer of them all the time.

The *Buffalo News* is the regional newspaper where, until
2012, I served as top editor for thirteen years. It's the largest
news organization in New York State outside the New York
City metro area. Like virtually every other newspaper in the
United States and many around the world, it's struggling. In the
internet age, circulation volume and advertising revenue have
plummeted, and the newsroom staff is less than half what it was
when I took the reins, down from two hundred to fewer than
a hundred journalists. That sounds bad, but is actually better
than most. American newspapers cut 45 percent of their newsroom staffs between 2008 and 2017, with many of the deepest
cutbacks coming in the years after that. In some places, the situation is far worse. (I use the term newspapers as a shorthand
for newspaper companies, and mean to include their digital, as
well as print, presence.)

It matters—immensely. As Tom Rosenstiel, executive director of the American Press Institute, put it: "If we don't monitor power at the local level, there will be massive abuse of power at the local level." And that's just the beginning of the damage that's already been done, with much more on the way. As a major PEN America study concluded in 2019: "As local journalism declines, government officials conduct themselves with less integrity, efficiency, and effectiveness, and corporate malfeasance goes unchecked. With the loss of local news, citizens are: less likely to vote, less politically informed, and less likely to run for office." Democracy, in other words, loses its foundation.

The decline of local news is every bit as troubling as the spread of disinformation on the internet. Cries of "fake news!" from President Trump and his sympathizers may seem like the biggest problem in the media ecosystem. It's true that the public's lack of trust in their news sources, sometimes for good reason, is a great worry. But intentional disinformation, media bias, and the disparagement of the press for political reasons are not the subjects of this book. While these may grab the public's attention, another crisis is happening more quietly. Some of the most trusted sources of news—local sources, particularly local newspapers—are slipping away, never to return. The cost to democracy is great. It takes a toll on civic engagement—even on citizens' ability to have a common sense of reality and facts, the very basis of self-governance. So I'll be clear: I'm not here to address the politicized "fake news" problem or the actual disinformation problem. This book is about the real-news problem.

"Welcome to Ground Zero," said Mark Sweetwood, managing editor of the *Youngstown Vindicator*, when I told him, in the

16   center of his newsroom (one that no longer exists), about the
book I was researching on the troubles of local news. I came to
the Ohio city only four days after a stunning announcement
that an already battered community took like a sucker punch:
Their daily newspaper was going out of business. August 31,
2019, would be the last day it published.

The *Vindicator* is far from alone. More than two thousand
American newspapers have closed their doors and stopped
their presses since 2004. And many of those that remain are
mere shadows of their former selves. Consider Denver, where
the *Denver Post* and the *Rocky Mountain News* boasted six hundred journalists twenty years ago—a robust group to cover a
city, surrounding metro area, and much of Colorado as a whole.
Both papers won Pulitzer Prizes. That situation has changed
radically. The "Rocky," as it was known, went out of business in
2009. And the *Denver Post*, owned by a hedge fund fronted by a
group called Digital First Media, is down to under seventy in its
newsroom. "It's painful—there's a knot in my gut to see what we
built up over time torn down in this relentless way," Greg Moore
told me in 2018. He was the *Post*'s top editor from 2002 to 2016,
when he stepped away, disheartened by what he called the ownership's "harvesting strategy."

My old paper, the *Buffalo News*, is facing an existential
threat. It lost money in 2018 for the first time in decades. This
development was frightening to its employees and management, though unknown to almost all local residents. Why would
they think the paper was hurting? After all, there were so many
years that the *News* would send a million dollars a week to its
Omaha-based owner, Warren Buffett's Berkshire Hathaway.
(Until early 2020, Berkshire owned dozens of papers, including

the *Omaha World-Herald*.) And though Buffett, who bought the
paper in the 1970s, says he loves newspapers, he had made it
clear that he was not inclined, over the long term, to support
papers that are losing money. He believes in the purpose of journalism but is not a newspaper philanthropist; the interests of
Berkshire's shareholders come first. And the famed investor is
extremely bearish about the future of local newspapers.

"They're going to disappear," Buffett said in a 2019 interview with Yahoo Finance. In a particularly memorable descrip-
tion, he said the newspaper business over the past few decades
"went from monopoly to franchise to competitive to . . . toast."
It's not hard to see the results of that trend: From 2004 to
2015, the U.S. newspaper industry lost over 1,800 print outlets as a result of closures and mergers, a study in the *Newspaper
Research Journal* found. Since then, the pace has only quickened,
and the future looks grimmer still. These days, there are hundreds of counties in America with no newspaper or meaningful
news outlet at all, creating "news deserts," as they've become
known. And many of those that do remain are "ghost newspapers"—phantoms of the publications they once were, and not
much good to the communities they purport to serve.

New York Times executive editor Dean Baquet joined his
voice to the dirge a few weeks after Buffett's interview, with
even more specific doom-predicting: "I think most local newspapers in America are going to die in the next five years, except
for the ones that have been bought by a local billionaire," he
told an audience at the International News Media Association
World Congress.

But, there's a serious perception problem—American citizens don't know about what's happening to local news, or

18   they choose not to believe it. As with issues like the global cli-
mate emergency, it is hard to convince a significant chunk of
the public that they ought to care deeply about this, or do anything about it. There are plenty of news sources—free, after
all—on the internet, though relatively few that dig into local
news with the skill of seasoned newspaper reporters like Barbara O'Brien. People may believe that their Facebook friends
will tell them what they need to know, without the benefit
of professional reporting. Their thinking seems to go something like this: News will find me if it's important enough. A
Pew study in 2019 astonished many journalists, who live with
the ugly reality of their drain-circling news business: Most
Americans—almost three of every four respondents—believe
that local news outlets are in good financial shape. And fewer
than one in six Americans actually pays for local news, which
includes having a subscription, print or digital, to the local
newspaper. Apparently, only a small percentage of the public
sees the need to open their wallets for their local newspapers
or other local news sources, and they aren't accustomed to
doing so. As newspapers decline in staff and quality, they see
even less reason to do so. Overcoming those factors is a steep
climb—with very little time to crest the hill.

Since becoming the media columnist for the *Washington
Post*, I've made it a practice to talk to local news consumers
wherever I travel. Often, the takeaway is not encouraging. Many
of the people I've interviewed, or simply chatted with, are dis-
enchanted with their local news sources. They see local TV
news as frothy—empty calories. Many of them mostly watch it
for the mainstays of weather and sports. What about the local
newspaper or its website, if they have one? It's a shadow of what

it once was, they often observe; it doesn't cover as much as it used to, and it seems to be chasing clicks most of the time. They also complain bitterly about inaccuracy or political bias—either seeing the paper as in the pocket of local business or, frequently, too far to the left (occasionally, too far to the right).

A Northern California man named Jeffrey Miller emailed me after I'd written a column about the withering of the Denver papers. Miller wanted to explain that he was struggling with his own conscience about maintaining a subscription to his greatly diminished local newspaper, the *San Jose Mercury News*, which is owned by the profit-sucking Digital First Media, controlled by Alden Global, a hedge fund: "The paper has become almost useless to me, and it feels like paying for it is only helping a hedge fund instead of advancing journalism." Miller said he would sometimes see articles repeated in the same edition, that sports coverage from the night before rarely made it into the paper, and that the quality of the reporting overall had dropped precipitously. There were a few local columnists he still enjoyed reading, but that was about the extent of it. The *Mercury News*, once a powerhouse local paper, owned by the high-quality Knight-Ridder chain, with a staff of more than three hundred journalists, has changed almost beyond recognition. Miller asked me whether I thought he should quit or keep subscribing. I sympathized with his quandary, but asked him to stick with the paper, despite his legitimate complaints. As I explained, the *Merc*, even in its enervated state, is probably the only hope for regularly covering city and county government and the public schools, and for maintaining something of a "village square" for the region. Miller, who is an avid news consumer and subscribes to national newspapers, agreed that he would do so, at least

20   temporarily. But many subscribers make a different decision: They bail out. And their departure perpetuates the problem that seems to have no answer, but that does have a serious cost to citizenship and democracy.

When local news fails, the foundations of democracy weaken. The public, which depends on accurate, factual information in order to make good decisions, suffers. The consequences may not always be obvious, but they are insidious.

The tight connection between local news and good citizenship became abundantly clear in 2018 for Nate McMurray, the Democratic candidate for Congress in a heavily Republican district in western New York. Although McMurray, the supervisor of the town of Grand Island, was battling a party enrollment skewed against him (the district is the size of Rhode Island and spreads into eight counties), he did have one monumental advantage: His Republican opponent, incumbent congressman Chris Collins, had just been indicted on insider-trading charges. One would think that would be disqualifying. News of Collins's indictment did make a difference in the election, especially in the parts of the district where local news was strong. The *Buffalo News*'s Washington correspondent, Jerry Zremski, had broken the insider-trading story and the paper followed developments diligently for months. Many who would likely have voted for the incumbent crossed the aisle to vote blue. But that wasn't always the case in the more far-flung parts of the district, ones less served by strong local news.

The problem, as McMurray saw it, was that in some parts of the sprawling congressional district, voters were shockingly uninformed. The largely rural and suburban district includes Orleans County. It was identified by the University of North

Carolina's Penny Muse Abernathy, probably America's leading
expert on the subject, as a "news desert," a rare one in New
York State.

"I'd be going door to door, or meeting with people at a
diner or a fair, for example, and in the most isolated areas, a
lot of people had no idea that their own congressman had been
indicted," McMurray told me. Orleans County was, he said, "one
of the toughest places." Some people didn't even know who Collins was, but many were incredulous when he told them of the
federal charges.

"People told me I was making it up," said McMurray. That
shouldn't have been the case, given that both Rochester and Buffalo television news were giving plenty of airtime to the scandal
as it developed, and those stations were available throughout
the district. But there was a time when almost everyone in the
district had ready access to the print editions of the *Rochester
Democrat and Chronicle*, a Gannett paper, or the *Buffalo News*, or
were within easy reach of smaller local papers.

Meanwhile, Collins, the first member of Congress to
endorse Donald Trump for president, was taking full advantage of the decline of credible news sources. He sent fundraising
emails to constituents blasting what he called "fake news" about
his misdeeds, and relied heavily on TV ads to get the message
out about his supposed effectiveness in Congress. McMurray
put it this way: "The lack of real journalism in a lot of the more
remote parts of the district meant that people were relying on
gossip, conservative radio, or social media. People were really
deep into their echo chambers, or they just didn't care."

McMurray ended up losing the 2018 election by a whisker—
less than half a percentage point. As for incumbent Chris

22 Collins, he pleaded guilty to two felonies, resigned from Congress, and was sentenced to prison. Some of his former constituents may be unaware of that, too, or wouldn't believe it if they saw it in a neighbor's Facebook post.

It's a vicious cycle—and one that has drawn the interest of researchers who have found that lack of trusted, factual information can lead to an overall decline of civic engagement. A *Journal of Politics* study showed that people in districts with weaker local coverage were less likely to be politically engaged and less likely to share opinions about the candidates running or give evaluations of their current representatives. Voting becomes more politically polarized when local news fades, says a study published in 2018 in the *Journal of Communication*— citizens are less likely to vote a split ticket, choosing candidates from various political parties. Instead, relying on national sources of news, including cable news outlets, they are more likely to retreat into tribal corners, voting along strict party lines.

It's not just about voting. It's about tax dollars. When local reporting waned, municipal borrowing costs went up, and government efficiency went down, according to a 2018 Hutchins Center working paper titled "Financing Dies in Darkness? The Impact of Newspaper Closures on Public Finance." A dearth of watchdog reporting has dire and quite specific results: "Following a newspaper closure, municipal borrowing costs increase by 5 to 11 basis points, costing the municipality an additional $650,000 per issue. This effect is causal and not driven by underlying economic conditions. The loss of government monitoring resulting from a closure is associated with higher government wages and deficits, and increased likelihoods of costly advance re-fundings and negotiated sales." What the researchers found was something we know intuitively but they found to be quantifiable: "Local newspapers hold their govern-ments accountable, keeping municipal borrowing costs low and ultimately saving local taxpayers money."

The harm is not confined to the United States. Studies in Japan and Switzerland have found much the same dynamic: In places where news breaks down, so does citizenship; where newspaper market share increases, so does political account-ability. The journalists I talked to or corresponded with in Brazil, in Italy, in Great Britain, in Canada, and elsewhere were worried about these industry trends and the fallout for the public, too.

This book will tell the most troubling news-media story of our time: how democracy suffers when local journalism fades. Through reporting in some of the so-called news deserts (or those stricken by "news poverty," as one researcher put it) around the United States—places with little or no local news— it will show the contours of the damage. And though I cannot fully answer the question of how to solve the problem, if indeed there is a solution, I will also look at the range of what is hap-pening in this environment: the rise of nonprofit news organiza-tions, the efforts of local public radio, the cooperation between large national news organizations and small local outlets. But for most newspapers, at least, the change is simple: continual decline with no end in sight.

There are exceptions. Some metropolitan areas—for exam-ple, the twin cities of St. Paul and Minneapolis, Minnesota— have relatively healthy local-journalism ecosystems. There are some encouraging signs in Boston. And there are bits of what looked like good (or less clearly bad) news, as some legacy newspapers met unexpected fates. At the *Los Angeles Times*, a

24 local billionaire bought the paper in 2018, providing hope to an important news source that had been buffeted by bad management and deep cutbacks. Its editor, Norman Pearlstine, began rebuilding it. (But even there, a year after that heralded purchase, the good news was not unalloyed. A critically important effort to gain and keep digital subscribers got off to a slow start before picking up steam in 2020.) The *New Orleans Times-Picayune*, whose coverage of Hurricane Katrina had been so vital in 2005 and beyond, had yielded suddenly to its upstart competitor in Baton Rouge, the *Advocate*, announcing that it would cease to exist as it had since 1837. The paper's historic name would live on, though, as the more-aggressive *Advocate* took it over and made its presence known in the Crescent City, hiring some of the *Times-Picayune*'s staff.

Innovative efforts to keep local news alive in a postnewspaper age are having some success—from impressive, nonprofit digital sites like MinnPost in Minnesota or Voice of San Diego to a fast-growing effort called Report for America, modeled partially on the Peace Corps, that puts hundreds of young journalists in underserved areas or hollowed-out newsrooms.

This is not by any means a strictly American phenomenon—far from it, since the effects of technology and the disappearing business model for traditional media sources do not agree to stay within arbitrary geographical boundaries.

Nostalgia is not the point here. There is no turning back the clock to pre-internet days when one-paycheck families watched the network evening news and got two dailies delivered, one before breakfast, one in the late afternoon. Another paean to the roar of rumbling presses, or to the glorious sound of print-advertising dollars ringing the cash register, does no good. Rather, what follows is intended to survey the damage and to sound a loud alarm, alerting citizens to the growing crisis in local news that has already done serious harm to our democracy: further polarizing our society, providing less incentive to vote, and failing to keep public officials accountable.

This story is not only about newspapers, though they are central to the narrative because their presence or absence affects so much of a region's news. Local television and radio are important, though their challenges are different in nature, often the result of the consolidation of ownership under corporations whose leadership doesn't care about journalism very much. As UNC's Abernathy told me bluntly: "We are seeing a collapse of the local news ecosystem." If she and Warren Buffett and Dean Baquet are right, if local newspapers are on the brink of extinction, with no adequate replacement in sight, citizens ought to know the extent of the losses now, before it's entirely too late. While Buffett said that most newspapers were "toast" because "the world has changed hugely," I don't believe that new technology is necessarily the answer. Online news sites have not been consistently better at capturing digital advertising revenue or convincing users to pay for content. In the internet age, information is largely free and many don't want to pay for it. Newspapers used to supply weather, comics, horoscopes, classifieds, and crosswords to get readers to pay for news, but even when the new digital-only news sites stripped away those add-ons, a leaner, meaner product has not always been more efficient, attractive, or lucrative. They still only represent a small portion of the industry, employ a fraction of out-of-work journalists, and cannot claim to have done a substantially better job at uncovering the news.

26   This is not to say that all local papers practice high-quality journalism. Some, and not just the smallest, are little more than the so-called "penny-savers," doing journalism by press release. Others suffer from lack of staff. One reader in Texas emailed me an image of the September 1, 2019, edition of the *Abilene Reporter-News*, which featured a flattering piece about a local accounting firm on its front page with a huge headline: "Condley & Co. at 80: Reputation Paramount." The photo was a lineup of eight smiling employees, with a framed portrait of the firm's founder on a table. My correspondent's comment was pithy: "When you live in a city with a daily newspaper and still live in a news desert." It brought to mind an axiom: "Journalism is what somebody doesn't want you to know. The rest is advertising." Still, I'd wager that many of the readers of the *Reporter-News* would be sorry to lose their daily paper, which offers sports, obituaries, and other valuable coverage—and I hope they don't. At the core, this book is about a once-profitable industry that was able to support an important public function but is now no longer profitable. We need to find other ways to support that function, or hope that consumers or other sources will be persuaded to pay for or subsidize that service somehow.

Reporting this book meant chronicling a situation that was quickly and constantly deteriorating. Huge media chains were merging, more newspapers were going out of business, digital sites were being abruptly axed, journalists continued to be laid off, not just at newspapers but at digital-first news companies that once were considered the rightful heirs to old-style print. When the coronavirus hit in early 2020, the immediate economic impact on news organizations could be felt worldwide. Advertising, already sparse, almost disappeared for some.

By late March, newspapers in Australia and Great Britain had folded or suspended printing. In the United States and elsewhere, new rounds of layoffs or pay cuts devastated the very local newsrooms that were making themselves more vital than ever to their readers by covering the burgeoning public-health emergency. But even before this disaster happened, the harsh consequences were playing out in communities. Meetings of public officials took place without coverage. Agency budgets and municipal contracts went forward without scrutiny. Readers, unhappy with news coverage or financially strapped because they had lost their jobs, decided to end their subscriptions. Despite some hopeful signs, the ghosting of local news was happening before my eyes—fast, and with no end in sight.

Leaving Buffalo

In the summer of 2019, with a certain amount of trepidation, I attended a summer party at the *Buffalo News*. It would be the first time I'd been back in the newspaper building since I stepped down as editor in 2012 to become the public editor of the *New York Times*. When I arrived, I found a festive scene. Cocktails and oysters were served on a balcony overlooking the Lake Erie harbor and the new construction at the city's Canalside development, which housed shops, restaurants, and, in winter, a skating rink near the arena where the Buffalo Sabres played their NHL games. Buffalo, once the eighth largest city in the United States and the bustling eastern terminus of Great Lakes shipping until the St. Lawrence Seaway came along in 1959, had fallen on hard times when the steel and auto plants hit the skids in the 1980s. The Bethlehem Steel plant in Lackawanna, the small city just south of Buffalo where I was born and raised, was once the largest steel factory in the nation, employing twenty thousand workers. It shut down in 1982, leaving a huge, largely abandoned industrial carcass on the Lake Erie waterfront.

But in recent years, Buffalo has bounced back economi-
cally and has become an unlikely darling of tourism roundups of
coolest cities to visit. It landed on a list of "best places for mil-
lennials to settle," and my son, a young public defender, was one
of them. He lives in a rehabbed industrial building downtown,
where the high ceilings and low rents are the envy of his coastal
friends. Whether Buffalo's resurgence has benefited the city's
large poor population was far less certain.

Inside the newspaper building, as I feared, the changes were
breathtaking. Home to a thousand employees not so long ago, it
now employed less than half of that. Chatting with my former
colleagues on the executive committee and others in the know,
I heard nothing encouraging. These conversations left me with
the depressing sense that the paper, even if it endured, would
be vastly changed over the next five years. Its staff likely would
continue to shrink and it might eventually publish in print only
on Sundays, if at all. It was tough to hear, but it resonated with
everything I knew from covering the national media scene for
the *Washington Post*.

Still, this was personal. This was where I had grown up,
written thousands of stories, met and married another reporter
when we were in our twenties, won writing awards, hired scores
of journalists, and even hopped in an ambulance when a preg-
nant reporter went into labor. It was in this building's first-floor
auditorium that the newsroom's journalists gave me a standing
ovation when I was named the paper's first female managing
editor. That was one of the great thrills and honors of my life. In
short, this was my world. And it was suffering. For several weeks
in every recent summer, I've moved back to the Buffalo area and
worked from a family cottage, always arranging immediately for

30 home delivery of the paper. It would land on my front deck in its orange plastic bag by 6 a.m. most mornings. The idea hit me hard that perhaps next summer—or the following one—that would no longer be possible.

That notion was just about unimaginable for me. After all, I had spent an entire professional lifetime there. As I prepared to emerge from Northwestern University's Medill School of Journalism with my newly minted master's degree in 1980, I was lucky enough to have summer internship offers at both of my hometown papers, the morning *Buffalo Courier-Express* and the *Buffalo Evening News*. I wasn't sure what to do, so I put the question to my father, a Buffalo defense attorney. I remember his words: "The *News* is the dominant paper." Dominant sounded good; I took the *News* internship. My mother, eager for me to stay local at the end of the summer tryout, used some equally memorable words as she pushed me to excel and to make my presence known to the powers-that-be. "Ingratiate yourself," she said. I didn't like the sound of that. I wanted to be known for my journalism, not for my winning personality. At any rate, and for whatever reason, when September came, I was offered a full-time reporting job on the business desk. I thought I would stick around Buffalo for a couple of years and move on— perhaps to the *Boston Globe* or the *Chicago Tribune*—but that never happened. I stayed, moving up the ranks and doing nearly every job in the newsroom. I got married, bought a house, had two children, and eventually, in 1999, became its first female top editor. It had taken me nineteen years to go from summer intern to executive editor, a job I would hold for nearly thirteen years before moving to New York City. And I appreciated the privilege every day as editor. As J. D. Salinger's fictional Buddy Glass said about entering the classroom where he taught undergraduates, to me that newsroom was a patch of holy ground that I was fortunate to walk on every working day.

The paper, like many another regional dailies of that era, was stable and financially solid for most of that period. Before I had arrived, the *News* was bought by Warren Buffett and became part of his Berkshire Hathaway empire. But Buffett knew that the Buffalo market could support only one daily; cities all over the country were seeing the shuttering of the second or third paper in town.

So Buffett, through his appointed publisher Stanford Lipsey and then-editor Murray Light, set about making sure the winner in Buffalo would be the *News*. (Lipsey had sold his chain of weeklies, Sun Newspapers, to Buffett in the late 1960s, remaining as publisher; a few years later, he enlisted Buffett's help in conceptualizing a story that eventually won a Pulitzer Prize for local investigative reporting on financial malfeasance at Omaha's Boys Town charity.) In Buffalo, Lipsey's and Light's paper competed fiercely for further market domination, starting a Sunday edition to go head to head with the *Courier*. They won the newspaper war in Buffalo. In 1982, the *Courier-Express* published its last edition. The *Buffalo News* dropped "Evening" from its nameplate, began a morning edition, and became exactly what Buffett wanted it to be, from a business perspective: the only game in town. At its peak, Sunday circulation was about 350,000, and the paper boasted the highest market penetration of any regional paper in the United States.

The paper hired some of the best talent from the *Courier*, including political cartoonist Tom Toles, who would win the *News* its third Pulitzer Prize. (When Toles left to replace the

32   legendary Herbert Block at the *Washington Post*, I had the sense
to hire one of our interns, Adam Zyglis, a talented cartoonist
and illustrator, fresh out of Buffalo's Canisius College. I urged
him to do the kind of work that would win a Pulitzer. He prom-
ised me that he would, and in 2015, he delivered on the promise.)
The *News* even hired the *Courier*'s executive editor, Douglas
Turner, and installed him as the paper's Washington bureau
chief. With bureaus all around the western end of the state and a
strong presence in Albany and Washington, the *News* was a solid
and well-respected newspaper.

And for years, it had what seemed like a license to print
money. Like other monopoly newspapers, its profit margins
were well above 30 percent. But it kept a relatively lean staff,
something I tried to change when I became editor. I didn't get
very far in terms of increasing the numbers, but I was successful
in another goal: to diversify the staff, which was far too white
for a city like Buffalo. I aggressively hired people of color; pro-
moted an editorial writer, Rod Watson, to be the first black
editor in newsroom management; and made Dawn Bracely the
first black woman on the editorial board. After the *News* bought
badly needed new presses in 2004, the paper's design director,
John Davis, redesigned the entire paper; the elegant new look
won a slew of national awards. I started the paper's first investigative team, and focused the staff's journalism on inequality
in the public schools and poverty in the city, where more than
two of every five children lived below the poverty line. I tangled
with Mayor Byron Brown over access to government information, and he wasn't sorry to see me leave town when the time
came. Our watchdog reporting was aggressive, and we got sued
from time to time, but we never lost or even settled a case.

Then came 2008. It would turn out to be a terrible year for newspapers, followed by many more terrible years in a row. The country's financial crisis and the recession that followed meant bad things for the industry. Print advertising, our life-blood and largest revenue source, dried up. Circulation, the second greatest source of revenue, fell. And there was no work-able strategy for the digital future. The rarely updated website was free, and digital advertising didn't begin to make up for the loss of print ads.

I remember sitting in endless meetings with other mem-bers of the executive committee. I kept trying to make the case that cutting the newsroom staff was the wrong way to save money. But to some, cutting jobs seemed like the most effective way to stay in the black. Because most of the newsroom staff belonged to the Newspaper Guild, layoffs would have meant losing the most recent hires. Instead, we began rounds of vol-untary buyouts, offering some of the most valuable and expe-rienced staffers money to go away. After years of trying to get the newsroom staff above its set point of 200, I had to reconcile myself to going in the opposite direction. By the time I left in 2012, the newsroom staff was below 150. But I took a measure of pride and satisfaction in avoiding layoffs; those who left did so of their own volition, knowing that taking a buyout might be the best opportunity to retire early with some extra cash, or start a new career with a cushion of time.

But the smaller staff meant we had to make some tough decisions about coverage. No longer would we have one reporter for suburban schools and one for the city schools. No longer would we have satellite bureaus in western New York's most

34   populous suburbs, where citizens could walk in with a tip or a complaint. The Washington bureau, which for years had two full-time reporters, a year-round intern, and an oversized office in the National Press Building, was eventually pared down to one reporter who worked from his home. Our Sunday magazine was reduced to a monthly, and then put out of business altogether, a particularly wrenching decision because my then-husband was the magazine's editor. No longer could we afford a full-time art critic or a full-time classical music critic. We cut way back on assignments that required travel. We thought these measures amounted to austerity at the time, and in comparison to a decade earlier, they seemed drastic. But things would get far worse.

After I departed, the entire copy desk would be dismantled, a move that many newspapers were making to streamline their skinnier operations. And the arts coverage, so important to Buffalo's rich cultural life, withered away. There were no more staff-written movie or book reviews, no more daily "Life & Arts" section. The paper's role as the center of the city's cultural life was fading. After all, a newspaper's purpose isn't only to keep public officials accountable; it is also to be the village square for an entire metropolitan area, to help provide a common reality and touchstone, a sense of community and of place.

For me, these changes really hurt. For whatever the cost to individuals on the staff, the cost to citizens was far worse. A city that had two thriving and competing papers in the early 1980s was down to one that was hemorrhaging talent and its boots-on-the-ground reporting. Buffalo still had three television stations—affiliates of CBS, NBC, and ABC—as well as a public radio station and a twenty-four-hour cable news channel. But none of them was built to provide the type of coverage long found in the *Buffalo News*: granular beat and community reporting, serious arts coverage, and wide-ranging account-ability journalism. "Do more with less" became a bitter industry joke. Worthy local reporting requires time, expertise, talent, and institutional knowledge. We had less of those every month, and the readers knew it. Perhaps paradoxically, I was immensely proud of the work we did and the overall quality of the paper. I felt that way until my last day on the job in August 2012, and I remain proud to be associated with the paper, which has continued to do vital work. The day I left the *Buffalo News*, I sat on the bare desk in my cleared-out office, and staff photographer Harry Scull came in to shoot a final portrait before we walked over to my farewell party on the fantail of the U.S.S. *Little Rock*, docked in Buffalo harbor. It was thirty-two years after I'd walked through the door as an ambitious summer intern, and everything—everything—had changed.

The Unregulated Toll Bridge

In 1977, shortly after Warren Buffett bought the *Buffalo Evening News* for $33 million, the *Wall Street Journal* quoted a Wall Street investor familiar with the so-called Sage of Omaha's thinking about newspaper economics. David Gottesman, senior partner of First Manhattan Corp., described it thus:

> Warren has been largely restricting himself to companies which he feels offer some protection against inflation in that they have a unique product, low capital needs, and the ability to generate cash. For example, Warren likens owning a monopoly or market-dominant newspaper to owning an unregulated toll bridge. You have relative freedom to increase rates when and as much as you want.

At that time, the *Buffalo News* was far from a monopoly. It was in head-to-head competition with the *Courier-Express*, the morning paper, which had a strong Sunday edition; the *News*'s flagship product came on Saturday afternoon each week.

In the 1970s and 1980s, most cities could support only one
newspaper. My uncle had been managing editor of the *Cleveland
Press*, which, after his retirement, lost its city's newspaper battle
to the *Cleveland Plain Dealer*. The *Press* went out of business in
1982. (And these days, the once-robust *Plain Dealer* is down to a
skeleton staff, like so many other metro dailies.)

So, yes, Buffett won the newspaper war in Buffalo, and the
paper's financial performance was everything he could have
wished for. For decades, it boasted profit margins well over
30 percent. Like an unregulated toll bridge, it was able to raise
advertising rates almost at will, or at least to keep up with infla-
tion and other rising costs.

Then came the internet. For many years, if you wanted
to sell something, the local newspaper was your best bet to
get the word out to potential buyers. A boat, a bike, a car you
wanted to unload? Put it in the advertisements at the back of
the daily paper that were divided into subject categories. Classified advertising was a big chunk of the newspaper's revenue,
and because there were few alternatives (fliers stuck under
neighbors' doors or posted on a church bulletin board?), newspapers could charge plenty for the service—and they did.
Department stores and car dealers and supermarkets took out
big display ads or special sections. The money poured in. But
something was happening in San Francisco that would change
all that. A tech entrepreneur named Craig Newmark had started
an emailed newsletter in the mid-1990s, and then invented its
outgrowth, a website that allowed people to post their goods
and services, mostly for free, with a few lucrative exceptions. By
2006, according to *Forbes* magazine, Craigslist ranked seventh
among all websites in terms of monthly page views. And almost

38   immediately, newspapers felt the hit, one they never recovered from—though that blow alone would not have been enough to sink them.

(Interestingly, Newmark in recent years has become a philanthropist deeply devoted to helping quality journalism survive in the digital age, and to helping journalists with new-media issues of all sorts. The City University of New York's graduate school of journalism bears Newmark's name, recognizing his $20 million gift; and he has given millions to other worthy journalistic institutions or programs, including a new effort to address digital security and ethics at Columbia University's Graduate School of Journalism. And Newmark has opened his home in Manhattan's West Village for salon-like journalism gatherings where you might see former BuzzFeed editor Ben Smith, former *Guardian* editor Alan Rusbridger, and academic luminaries like Columbia University's Emily Bell. It's an outcome that no one could have predicted when the classifieds were falling away.)

An even more profound change was coming from two dominant technology platforms, Google and Facebook, who have been able to attract the vast portion of digital advertising. By some estimates, the "duopoly" was sucking up 60 percent of all digital advertising revenue in the United States by the middle of the last decade. From the point of view of traditional publishers, this seemed almost diabolical because the platforms benefited from "content"—the news stories, videos, photo galleries, etc.—that the old-school companies supplied, but siphoned off most of the revenue. That content (let's go ahead and call it journalism) is often expensive to produce. It requires, for example, skilled reporters digging through documents or

sitting in long government meetings, not always immediately
finding the meaty news they are seeking but having to put in the
effort anyway.

One key to the platforms' astonishing success in attracting
digital advertising was targeting, particularly in the case of
behemoth Facebook. Targeting means determining to a relatively narrow degree who would see a particular ad. Facebook
could control that closely and charge advertisers relatively
little. For its part, Google could "serve" or deliver advertising
when people did a search for a particular product. Advertisers
could also see how successful their efforts were, and they were
willing to pay a higher rate if they knew a particular ad or ad
campaign was leading to purchases. This was a big advantage
over print or television ads. And, of course, the platforms dominate online advertising because of the scale of their users. This
ubiquity, along with narrow targeting, was a tough combination
to compete against.

As the Reuters Institute succinctly put it in its 2018 study
of local newspapers in Europe, "Advertisers increasingly invest
in online advertising, which is dominated by large U.S. based
platform companies that offer low prices, precise targeting, and
unduplicated reach. Local newspapers cannot compete directly."
For these papers in France, Germany, Finland, and the United
Kingdom, "their traditional business model, advertising, is thus
existentially challenged."

For many decades, newspaper and television ads offered
the opposite of this targeting. Everyone reading the paper or
watching a TV show saw the same advertisement. (There were
exceptions but they were blunt instruments, not scalpels.
Zoned editions of newspapers might be considered a primitive

40   form of the targeting to come. If you lived in a city's northern suburbs, for example, you would see advertisements for stores in the northern suburbs.)

Writing in Recode, Kurt Wagner detailed a well-anticipated tipping point that came in 2019. Digital advertising was set to outpace "traditional" advertising such as printed ads for, say, supermarkets in newspapers or broadcast ads for cars on television. The Recode subheadline was straightforward: "TV and newspapers are out. Facebook and Google are in." Wagner wrote that the change had happened swiftly. "Even though digital advertising was just half the size of the 'traditional' ad industry four years ago in 2015, it was only a matter of time before the two swapped roles." Some 60 percent of digital advertising belonged to Facebook and Google together, amounting to $65 billion. The platforms, despite being under fire from would-be regulators and many, many critics, were hugely successful and becoming more so.

There was a time when newspaper publishers held onto a false hope: Digital advertising revenue would fill the gap left by the print ads that were slipping away so inexorably. Indeed, there is a tremendous amount of digital ad spending. The problem, though, is that most of the money wouldn't be going to content publishers, also known as news organizations. It would largely go to Facebook and Google, who were able to give advertisers cheap prices and a narrowly targeted audience. What's more, those platforms controlled the advertising networks that serve most of the ads one sees across the web.

But there was so much more to deal with than just the loss of advertising revenue. In the post-Vietnam and post-Watergate era, social habits were changing. With both parents in a typical middle-class family now working outside the home, there was less time for, and interest in, local papers. Freestanding department stores that were once dependable and deep-pocketed advertisers were first drawn into malls, and then slowly replaced by online shopping. Car dealerships began to reach their customers through targeted internet advertising or direct mail. Amazon was siphoning off the profits and potential ad dollars of local business.

When the 2008 financial crisis came, followed by the Great Recession, newspapers saw their advertising and circulation tumble. It's no exaggeration to say that revenue fell off a cliff, as a well-circulated graphic from the Newspaper Association of America made abundantly clear. From its peak in 2000 to 2012, print advertising fell 71 percent; digital advertising never made a serious difference in recovering the loss.

With fewer advertising dollars and less circulation, newspapers responded by cutting staff. It was the most immediate and easiest way to save money, and to keep profits relatively high. (Or, in some cases, just to try to stay profitable.) Round after round of layoffs and buyouts at nearly every paper in the country resulted; local journalists who thought they had a lifetime job covering local government, for example, were out on the street. Copyeditors were deemed nonessential. Unsurprisingly, the quality of many newspapers went down.

This was happening everywhere, at newspapers of every size. "We've had to make some tough decisions," said Ken Tingley, editor of the *Glens Falls Post-Star*, a Pulitzer Prize—winning daily in the Adirondacks region of New York. With his staff down by about half, he has been forced to reduce news coverage of the region and concentrate on the metro area.

What concerns Tingley even more is what happens to the journalism-talent pipeline, that there's not much of a career ahead for the young reporters on his staff. "Where are they going to go?" Tingley said, when bigger metro dailies keep shrinking their staffs. The career path that helped so many young journalists become superstars of their craft is mostly gone now. David Halberstam, one of the most revered reporters of the twentieth century, started out at the *Daily Times Leader* in West Point, Mississippi, the smallest daily newspaper in Mississippi, and then moved to the *Tennessean* in Nashville, before arriving at the *New York Times*, where his Vietnam War reporting distinguished him. *Washington Post* executive editor Marty Baron, who has been my boss since 2016 and is considered by many the greatest editor of his generation, began his career at the *Miami Herald* as a reporter in the Stuart, Florida, bureau, and then as a *Herald* business reporter. What's more, Baron may be best known for his role as executive editor of a regional newspaper, the *Boston Globe*, where he led the coverage of the sexual abuse scandal in the Catholic Church, as immortalized in the Oscar-winning film *Spotlight*. Halberstam, Baron, and countless others probably could not get their start that way anymore. And that is an incalculable loss.

Meanwhile, chain ownership of newspapers was on the rise. Once mostly the province of local families who ruled their media fiefdoms with a wide variety of wisdom or venality, and usually with at least a modicum of civic responsibility, newspapers began to be snapped up more and more by big corporations. Some of them, like Gannett or Knight-Ridder, which later gave way to the California-based McClatchy Company, were reasonably well run. They did right by readers while still making a

profit. Gannett was known for squeezing its newspaper properties by running them with lean staffs; Knight-Ridder had a more
expansive reputation. But in the all-new newspaper economy,
Gannett employees felt relatively fortunate, especially as one
of the most profit-hungry chains, GateHouse Media, swooped
in for a merger. The marriage of the largest and second-largest
chains would give the combined newspaper giant control
of one of every six newspapers in America. The author and
news industry analyst Ken Doctor, a longtime Knight-Ridder
employee, predicted that the deal would go through, but noted
that the merger had nothing to do with producing great journalism. "These companies' leaders think a mega merger buys
two or three years—'until we figure it out.' The 'it' is that long-
hoped-for chimera of successful digital transformation," he
wrote. "Gannett and GateHouse, like all their industry brethren,
look at ever-bleaker numbers every quarter; the biggest motiva-
tion here is really survival, which in business terms means the
ability to maintain some degree of profitability somewhere into
the early 2020s."

As fortunes turned downward in newspapers over the past
two decades, a new kind of ownership came along: private equity
firms whose management had no interest in journalism, but a
great deal of interest in strip-mining papers for whatever financial value they had left. As the unwelcome trend was reaching a
new peak, journalists Robert Kuttner and Hildy Zenger wrote a
sweeping account of this in 2017:

Companies with names like Alden Capital, Digital First
Media, Citadel, Fortress, GateHouse, and many others that
you've never heard of have purchased more than 1,500 small-

44   city dailies and weeklies. The malign genius of the private equity business model . . . is that it allows the absentee owner to drive a paper into the ground, but extract exorbitant profits along the way from management fees, dividends, and tax breaks. By the time the paper is a hollow shell, the private equity company can exit and move on, having more than made back its investment. Whether private equity is contained and driven from ownership of newspapers could well determine whether local newspapers as priceless civic resources survive to make it across the digital divide.

Alden Global, through its majority control of the management company known by the benign-sounding name of Digital First Media, was perhaps the worst of a bad lot. Its hundred or so newspapers include weekly and daily papers—including some once-major regional metro papers, like the *San Jose Mercury News* and the *Denver Post*.

In 2018, newsroom employees of some of those papers protested the destruction of journalism in their communities outside the so-called Lipstick Building in midtown Manhattan, where Alden Global is based. That effort proved futile, but they did draw attention to what was happening.

I found the Denver situation particularly poignant because of the precipitous fall from prominence of the city's journalism. I spoke to a young reporter, Jesse Aaron Paul, who told me that when he came to the *Denver Post* as a summer intern in 2014, "I felt like I had reached the end of the yellow brick road." In a reverent tone, Paul recalled his first day at the paper with its history of Pulitzer Prizes, its beautiful downtown building (it was, he said, "like a beacon"), and its nationally regarded top editor,

Greg Moore, who hired him at summer's end and, because of his
energy and productivity, dubbed him "Super Jesse."

Four years later, it had all come crashing down, as was so often the case when Alden Global was involved. One of Alden's trademark moves is to sell off the prime downtown property and move the newsroom operation somewhere much less glorious. Newsroom employees were summoned to an all-staff meeting at the paper's new headquarters, a printing plant in an outlying county. At this meeting, the staff believed that a small number of buyouts might be offered. They reasoned that there wasn't much left to cut, after so many employees had been laid off in recent years. But that was a miscalculation: Another thirty newsroom jobs would disappear. The news, Jesse Paul told me, was greeted by "sobs, gasps and expletives." It meant that the newsroom, which once numbered about three hundred positions, would drop to less than seventy. And since the *Post*'s competitor, the *Rocky Mountain News*, had gone under a decade before, that meant fewer than seventy people were left to cover all aspects of a major metropolitan area. (In 2018, the *Colorado Sun*, a newly formed newsroom made up of twelve former *Denver Post* employees, added to the local coverage; Jesse Paul has joined that newsroom's staff.)

Greg Moore described Alden Global's "harvesting strategy": Take whatever profits you can right now, and don't worry about future viability, or about journalism. "Just short of setting the place on fire, being bought by Digital First is about the worst outcome possible," Joshua Benton, director of the Nieman Journalism Lab at Harvard, wrote in the *Boston Globe* about Alden's purchase of the *Boston Herald* in 2018. "It's less the *Herald* being saved than the *Herald* being stripped for parts."

This was happening not just at Alden Global's newspapers but at those owned by GateHouse Media, another large chain, and in somewhat less drastic ways at papers owned by Gannett and McClatchy. In some cases, the news was even worse. One day in late June 2019, the 150-year-old family-owned *Vindicator* in Youngstown, Ohio, announced that it was shutting down in a matter of weeks. There was no middle ground of trying an all-digital approach, or deciding to cut certain days of print or home delivery. Youngstown would become the first substantial American city to have no daily paper.

The local-news environment is not without its bright spots. One of the most encouraging developments is the significant growth of public radio, and the collaboration among stations. In 2018, for example, ten stations across the United States, from Dallas to Atlanta, teamed up for a two-year reporting project on gun violence, with grant funding from a family foundation. And National Public Radio editorial director Nancy Barnes, in an interview with Poynter.org, said she envisioned adding more than one thousand local-news jobs, maybe double that. That's something that gets less attention than it should, and could make a significant difference in the overall local-news scene.

Local TV stations, for the most part, have seen revenues either stabilize or go on the upswing, though their viewership has declined as younger generations increasingly turn to their smartphones for news and information of all sorts. From a business perspective, they have a great advantage, reports Pew Research: Revenue from retransmission fees paid by cable and satellite systems to carry local channels has been increasing rapidly in the past decade. Using estimates from Kagan, a media research group, Pew noted that revenue from retransmission fees grew from $9.4 billion in 2017 to $10.2 billion in 2018, and would reach $12.2 billion by 2023. But will those billions be used to produce valuable journalism, or simply pocketed?

Some stations have found a competitive advantage in pursuing investigative reporting, or at least some version of it. "Stations need market differentiation—a distinction between what they offer and what everybody else offers," Al Tompkins, senior faculty member for broadcast at the Poynter Institute, told me. He observed, though, that not all of what TV stations tout as investigative journalism meets his definition. "A lot of investigative folks are doing 'day turns' and you have to ask: How investigative can you be in eight hours?"

"Stories about bedbugs that are called investigative journalism are kind of silly," said Sarah Cohen, who runs a data journalism team at the *New York Times*. "But not everything has to be a six-month project. The core of investigative work is something of public importance that somebody doesn't want you to know."

A 2018 Knight Foundation study called for local TV stations to improve their journalism: "Drop the obsession with crime, carnage, and mayhem. And focus on ways to connect with local communities through a focus on issues such as education, the economy, and transportation." The good news for local TV only seemed relatively positive because of an adjacent disaster: "In some ways, local TV news benefits because its competitors are so troubled. Newspapers have been losing circulation since long before the internet, revenues are plummeting, and many newspapers might not survive beyond the next few years."

If that revenue can be harnessed for good, TV can be a part of the answer. But it's unclear that it will be. Adam Symson, president and chief executive officer of E.W. Scripps Company, which owns sixty local television stations across the country, told me he isn't especially hopeful about putting the future of serious local journalism in the hands of the huge media companies that own most American stations: "There's an incredible opportunity to fill the gap created by the decline of newspapers, if we focus our attention on enterprise reporting and beat reporting." The staff size at many local television stations is no longer dwarfed by that at local newspapers, largely because newspaper staffs have shrunk so dramatically. "It's incumbent on local television to carry the mantle of accountability reporting," he said. As a former investigative TV journalist himself, Symson insisted that the Scripps stations and the company as a whole operate under the mantra of "journalism first." But "journalism first" is not the standard across the local-television industry, as many owners put profit first. "What we're seeing is the move of pure financial players into the television space," Symson said, "with the same motivations as the newspaper players," such as Digital First Media, which is essentially a hedge fund.

In order for local television news to meet its journalistic potential, he said, "we have to recast our product—to get away from stenography and move in the direction of enterprise reporting." And despite its relative financial health, local television is plagued by changes in consumer habits, as people of all ages move away from what was once the daily routine of tuning into the local news on television at 5:00 or 6:00 p.m., and then again at 11:00 p.m. In short, television journalism can be part of the answer to the crisis in local news, as newspapers struggle for survival and digital upstarts attempt to fill the void. Whether it will reach its potential is far less certain.

In 2020, even Warren Buffett was giving up on newspapers.
Over the decades, Berkshire Hathaway had amassed thirty-one
dailies and forty-nine weeklies. But in January, the corporation announced that it was exiting the industry and selling its
entire newspaper empire to Lee Enterprises, a publishing conglomerate that already owned fifty dailies and had been managing most of Berkshire Hathaway's print operations. Among
the papers being sold was, of course, the *Buffalo News*.

News Deserts, Ghost Papers, and Beacons of Hope

Youngstown, Ohio

The *Vindicator* newsroom had a decidedly 1980s feel—reporters had cubicles and there was run-down gray carpet and furniture. And it was emptied out. Just a few of the desks were occupied by editors or reporters, but the expansive size of the newsroom suggested that this had once been a bigger, more bustling place. Those who were there were working hard, and also having fun, in the dark, gallows-humor way that's typical of newsrooms. Mark Sweetwood, who commandeered a desk in the center of the newsroom, not sequestered in an office, was calling out assignments, deciding story lengths, and checking in with reporters. As I sat at one of the nearby desks, I could hear the familiar music of a typical newsroom: a blend of cynicism that cannot disguise a shared sense of mission, mixed with the rush of deadlines and worry about getting something wrong or otherwise missing a big story. Newsrooms run on plentiful caffeine, high anxiety, and sick jokes. I heard pained humor about the paper gearing up to cover its own funeral, and about deadlines that absolutely couldn't be extended since, pretty soon, there would be no place to put a delayed story. The paper was about to close its doors.

Sweetwood told me that he kept thinking about a mostly forgotten column he admired and had recently reread. It was written by the late columnist Mike Royko, a Chicago journalism icon, on March 4, 1978, when the *Chicago Daily News* was going out of business. Royko puzzled over why a good newspaper, which the *Daily News* surely was, couldn't make it. He concluded that public apathy and distraction were big factors. "In the Chicago area, 1.6 million people will turn on *Welcome Back Kotter*. About 2.1 million watch *Charlie's Angels*. *Wonder Woman* draws 939,000. There's a big market for mental cotton candy," Royko wrote. "But out of 7 million who live in *The Daily News* circulation area, only 315,000 of them thought one of the better papers in America was worth 15 inflationary cents. When a new dictator takes over a country, one of the first things he does is seize or close the newspapers. Apathy isn't as heavy-handed as a dictator. But it can get the same job done."

Sweetwood saw the parallels with the *Vindicator*. People just didn't care enough, he felt. But, of course, there was one huge difference. After the *Daily News*'s demise, Chicago would still have two other daily newspapers. (A fourth, *Chicago Today*, had folded less than four years earlier.) Youngstown? None.

That night, at a community forum in the local history center about the *Vindicator*'s impending death, residents cried, talked about what they would miss—the obituaries, the high school sports coverage, the competition for the area's greatest golfer—and tried to come up with ways to save the company. They shared memories of delivering the paper as kids or of

52 being featured in it for one reason or another. But, as one editor wondered with a dash of well-founded skepticism, what would happen if there had been a show of hands in that room to identify those who actually subscribed to the newspaper they said they would miss so much? Circulation, after all, had sunk to about 25,000 daily and 32,000 on Sunday, about a quarter of what it was in the late 1970s. And that was far from the worst of the *Vindicator*'s problems.

Advertising had fallen off radically in a market that never was particularly robust. An employee union at the paper had gone on strike for nine months in 2004, just as Craigslist was coming on strong, meaning that the paper's lucrative classified ads were drying up. The *Vindicator* never really recovered from that unfortunate confluence of events. And even at its height, the *Vindicator* was far less financially successful than most. Its best year was in 1989, the paper's general manager, Mark Brown, told me, but even then the profit margin was 17 percent. That would be hefty in some industries, but far less than the 30 percent or more margins enjoyed by many newspapers and chains, margins that endured through the 1990s. The *Vindicator* had lost money for twenty of the past twenty-two years before it announced its closing. That was not the norm for regional newspapers, many of which had remained at least marginally profitable through those years.

The decision was also devastating for Brown's mother, Betty Brown Jagnow, who served as the publisher, and still came in to the paper's office a few days a week, well into her eighties. The *Vindicator* had been owned and run by their family for 132 of its 150 years. "It's all we've ever known and all we ever wanted to do," Brown told me, in a quiet voice and with a downcast expression,

as we sat in his office, a converted storage room where bright
lights blazed on an array of filing cabinets. It was not a fancy publisher's digs. The paper had put most of its money into staffing
the newsroom. Its forty-four journalists were a relatively robust
staff for a paper of its circulation size; though greatly reduced,
the *Vindicator* had not been cut to the bone.

There was a time, Brown recalled, when the *Vindicator*
was able to send a staff reporter or a freelance stringer to every
municipal board meeting and every school board meeting in
the surrounding three-county area. "People knew that," he
said, "and they behaved." But that practice had been gradually
reduced over the years. The remaining staff was not nearly large
enough to provide that kind of coverage, but it was a lot better
than nothing.

Youngstown was the kind of region that badly needs that
journalistic scrutiny, and by many accounts, still is. Writing
in the *New Republic* in 2000, David Grann called Youngstown
"Crimetown, USA," as it was a hotbed of mafia activity and
political corruption. The *Vindicator*'s editorial page editor,
Bertram De Souza, had been at the paper for forty years, and
had helped to reveal the malfeasance by one of Youngstown's
native sons—the infamous James Traficant, who was expelled
from Congress and sent to jail after being convicted of racke-
teering, taking bribes, and using his staff to do chores on his
home and houseboat. "It is absolutely the kind of place that
needs watchdog reporting," De Souza told me, "and this newspaper was committed to exposing corruption." With the *Vindicator* gone, he said, there will be no other entity that will carry
on that practice; no one to follow up on tips from sources; no
one to examine public documents; no one to file Freedom of

54   Information requests or demand access to meetings that should be public but are kept secret; no one with lawyers on retainer to help fight public-access battles. Almost inevitably, corruption will flourish, and the people of Youngstown won't even realize what may be happening under their noses, De Souza said. "I'm scared for the community," Mark Brown said.

Who will cover and uncover the news in Youngstown with the *Vindicator* gone? There were some signs of hope. A local competitor in nearby Warren planned to expand its Youngstown offerings, as did the local *Business Journal*. Before the *Vindicator* stopped publication in late August, Mark Brown was able to take a small measure of satisfaction in one development. He had agreed to sell the *Vindicator*'s name and certain of its assets (including its list of subscribers) to the Ogden newspaper chain, which publishes the *Tribune Chronicle* in nearby Warren. This meant that while the *Vindicator* would still close up shop, and its employees would lose their jobs, an edition of the Warren paper called the *Vindicator* would be distributed. But the *Vindicator* was still dead. Sure, it was better than nothing, but in terms of thorough local coverage, probably not much better.

There were a few other developments that helped ease the pain. The highly respected national nonprofit ProPublica decided to fund one investigative journalist at a Youngstown news outlet, as part of their efforts to address the local-news crisis. ProPublica works with twenty-three local partners across the country and pays the salary and a stipend for benefits so news organizations can devote a full-time reporter to work on a government accountability reporting project for a year. ProPublica also offers editing support, as well as data, research, engagement, audience, and production/design assistance. "What's going on in Youngstown and the Mahoning Valley cries out for solid investigative reporting," said Stephen Engelberg, ProPublica's editor in chief. "We created the Local Reporting Network to fill that critically important need." The three Youngstown TV stations would also do their part. One of them is owned by the same family that had run the newspaper for a century and a half.

Maybe most promisingly, the newspaper chain McClatchy said it would start an all-digital news site in Youngstown, partly with funding from Google. It would be called Mahoning Matters. (The Mahoning Valley is the area surrounding Youngstown, and the name is meant to reflect the organization's intention to report regionally, beyond the city limits.) Mark Sweetwood, the former managing editor of the *Vindicator*, would be its only editor, and two former *Vindy* reporters would be the only full-time journalists in its small staff, along with a publisher, a business executive, and several freelance writers and photographers. Mahoning Matters was the first result of Compass Experiment, a McClatchy and Google partnership that describes itself as "a local news laboratory" founded "to explore new sustainable business models for local news." But the *Vindicator* had forty people in its newsroom, not four. The new publication would not be able to produce nearly as much local journalism, and the lack of a physical newspaper would exclude some of the *Vindicator*'s core readership, many of whom had told me how much they still valued the old-fashioned tactile experience of reading the daily product in print.

In February 2020, McClatchy announced that it was more than $700 million in debt, and filed for bankruptcy. Control of the company would be turned over to the hedge fund Chatham

56   Asset Management, but its thirty newspapers would presumably be kept afloat, although it most likely meant even more severe cost-cutting and possibly the shuttering of enterprises like Mahoning Matters. Digital sites, it turns out, present many of the same problems as ones exhibited by newspapers. How do you capture advertising revenue, convince users to pay for your service, and free yourself from the fickleness and meddling of owners and donors? So far, no business model has been able to fully overcome these conundrums.

East Lansing, Michigan
When there's no one to uncover the news, it might seem like there is no news to be uncovered. When there's no one to sniff out scandal, it might seem like there is no scandal. But in East Lansing, Michigan, one woman's radical approach to citizen-generated news found something quite different. "It's amazing—there's one scandal after another, if you look," Alice Dreger told me.

You couldn't call East Lansing a news desert, because the Gannett-owned *Lansing State Journal* was in the adjacent and much bigger city of Lansing. But Gannett has vastly cut its staff to stay profitable, and coverage of East Lansing's government pretty much went away. The newspaper would cover the university, but rarely devote any column inches to East Lansing's city government, schools, or neighborhood issues. "There was basically no news coverage here," Dreger recalls.

Dreger is not a journalist by training. She is a bioethicist and taught at East Lansing's Michigan State University as well as Northwestern University in Chicago. Her 2015 book, *Galileo's Middle Finger: Heretics, Activists, and the Search for Justice in Science*, recounts her activism and controversies surrounding intersex genital surgery. A *New York Times* book review called it "a splendidly entertaining education in ethics, activism, and science." But since professional journalists weren't covering her town, she and some other community members started a local "discussion list" online, which grew to include coverage of meetings, efforts to free up government documents, and long features about local issues. She even started training people about how to do basic community reporting. Her "news brigade," which today numbers about 140, consists of housewives, students, and retired people of all stripes. They are compensated very little for their efforts, about $50 per article. "If you have a city on fire, and there's no fire department, people have to grab buckets. We got people to realize here we had a city on fire," she said.

For the first few years, Dreger's brigade worked in a relatively casual way, as a "voluntary citizen-reporting project." As they got more dedicated and more organized, Dreger turned the effort into a nonprofit corporation in 2014. She called her website East Lansing Info. She hired a retired automotive engineer as the managing editor. She started fundraising, but kept expenses extraordinarily low. And, she said, about half of what the site does is government reporting, which is what wasn't being done before. She had to explain to readers why ELI wasn't covering the biggest story the city has had in years: the scandal over Michigan State University physician Larry Nassar, a team doctor for USA Gymnastics accused of sexually assaulting or molesting hundreds of young women and minors, who was convicted and sentenced to multiple prison terms totaling more than a hundred years. "When I saw that the BBC was showing

58   up, I realized that was not something we needed to be spending
       our time on," she reasoned. (Reporting by a different newspaper,
       the *Indianapolis Star*, helped uncover the scandal and put Nassar
       in prison.)

       In recent years, here's some of what ELI has dug up:

- A mercury spill was mishandled at the East Lansing waste-
  water treatment plant. (The city fired the whistleblower who
  revealed what was happening.)
- East Lansing had a secret $200 million pension debt, which
  was gigantic for such a small city. The revelations were a core
  issue in the defeat of a popular mayor, Nathan Triplett, in
  2015, in an election that drew high voter turnout.
- A retaining wall, built at public expense with federal Housing
  and Urban Development funds, was benefiting the city attorney's personal property. HUD later deemed it a misappropri-
  ation of funds and demanded the money be returned.
- The city was selling off a piece of municipal property on the
  online auctioning website eBay.
- "The air conditioner story," as it's become known, told of how
  city government effectively outlawed thousands of "noisy"
  home air conditioners based on a couple of complaints about
  one air conditioner.

       "People used to tell us, 'There's no there there, in East
Lansing,'" Dreger said. But the nonprofit, to some extent, has
changed that. "When you create a news brigade, it's amazing.
You find out there's a there there, and it's beautiful. And nutty.
It turns into home." And that fulfills one of the many intangibles

lost when local news fades—the sense of community, of place, the role of news organization as a kind of village square where people gather to share a common experience.

For Dreger, one of the most notable and surprising results of her experiment is the way a group of amateur reporters made East Lansing residents appreciative of professional journalism. "People didn't see news as a service, they saw it as a product," she said. But she has found that people, including those who work with her, "are having energetic conversations about the meaning and purpose of news. This has turned a lot of people into evangelists for news."

Remarkably, ELI has a budget of only $100,000 a year, an amount that wouldn't even cover two reporters' salaries and benefits in many legacy newsrooms. "Nobody wants to talk about expenses," Dreger told me. But she has found that it's possible to run a nontraditional news organization on a shoestring. She sees a gender component to this situation. Women, culturally, are accustomed to volunteering their time or working for very low wages, especially when it benefits their communities. Women make up the majority of the 140 community members who have been "turned into reporters."

Pflugerville, Texas
John Garrett is standing in a cavernous 32,000-square-foot room proudly showing me something bizarre in this day and age: his company's shiny new Goss presses. Garrett and his wife and business partner, Jennifer, believe in print, and they are convinced that the news industry's focus on chasing those elusive digital advertising dollars has contributed hugely to its demise.

60   "We're not digital first," Garrett said. The Garretts founded Community Impact in 2005 with one paid employee. When I visited in 2019, they had 230 employees, staffing 34 publications in 4 states, with more to come. Their newspapers are mailed, free, to everyone in the circulation area. The digital sites have no paywall.

"And every year we've given raises to everyone on staff," he said, another rarity in the newspaper business. Reporters mostly make around $30,000 a year, some closer to $40,000. The company had never had a layoff despite starting up just a few years before the economic downturn and recession that brought an advertising collapse that decimated the news business. Community Impact had been moderately profitable almost every year, at about a 5 percent profit margin, Garrett said.

If Community Impact sounds like it takes a "penny-saver" approach to news, that's misleading. The full-color tabloid-size papers are "stitched and trimmed," meaning they are neatly edged and stapled, creating a high-end look. Though their staffs are tiny, the papers engage in true enterprise reporting on subjects like homelessness, road projects, taxes, and teacher salaries. They don't do what Garrett calls the kind of "Johnny kicked a field goal" coverage that characterizes most giveaway papers and many subscription-based weeklies, but they may occasionally do a feature on a local business. Advertisers aren't off limits for editorial coverage; but they're also not the only ones to get some ink, as a *Forbes* profile of the company noted. "I can't tell you how many people have told us we are their only real source of news, and that means a lot to us," Garrett told me. "We see that as a big part of our mission."

Its business model relies firmly on serving small, local advertisers by allowing them to reach very specific audiences in print. "I can honestly look advertisers in the eye and say we can compete with Facebook as far as targeting audiences," Garrett told me. The ads are specific to individual mail-carrier routes, and include restaurants, dentist offices, and hospitals. It has turned out to be a lucrative business. But expanding the company hasn't come without some scary moments. Probably the worst was the decision to spend $5 million on new presses at a time when conventional wisdom said that print was over and done with. "Dead trees," as the scornful dismissal went.

"I visited Long Island to see the new Goss Magnum Compact presses. On my way, I prayed and asked God to make it really clear we should make this kind of investment," Garrett told me. "I mean, I needed a clear sign." He got it. Just after his return, the *Austin American-Statesman* announced it would be shuttering its presses, and would print the paper from a remote location. For Garrett, it meant that his instinct was correct. He couldn't depend on another printer (in this case, the *Statesman*) to do their printing work. "We had to own our production." Later, he realized there was another, equally important reason that this mattered. "I didn't understand how important these skilled people were to the production process." It has been a big part of Community Impact's success. "The profits we have moved from outsourcing to insourcing are fueling our growth."

Community Impact combined its monthly, free, direct-mailed newspapers with a frequently updated news page on the web. The company isn't really a model for daily newspapers that are in trouble. But Garrett's approach was a recognition that

62   print advertising is still sustainable. More broadly, print still matters, even in the digital world. This print-advertising-based model, though, is especially susceptible to economic downturns like the one that accompanied the spread of the coronavirus. By March of 2020, advertising revenue had plunged deeply, and the company's executives were taking pay cuts while they tried to stave off staff layoffs and while they considered reducing some of their editions.

Garrett thinks that dailies are likely to move to Sunday-only in print and digital the rest of the week, which is precisely what another against-the-grain thinker has planned at the *Arkansas Democrat-Gazette* in Little Rock.

Little Rock, Arkansas

In mid-2019, the iconoclastic Walter E. Hussman Jr., publisher and owner of the *Arkansas Democrat-Gazette,* was doing something very unusual, as he was wont to do. The seventy-two-year-old was giving away $12 million worth of free iPads to his subscribers across the state. The idea was that they would be able to read, in digital form, what looked exactly, page by page, like a daily print edition, while the *Democrat-Gazette* moved actual print publication for most of its readers to one day a week, on Sundays.

I had been watching Hussman's against-the-grain moves for years, with admiration. In 2019, he gave $25 million to the University of North Carolina and became the namesake for the Hussman School of Journalism and Media; as part of the deal, he insisted that "journalism" and not "media" would come first in the official name. I heard him speak at a newspaper editors conference in the early 2000s, where he talked about why he'd put up a hard paywall at the paper after a two-year experiment in offering it free online. When I asked him about it in an interview, he recalled the experience of hearing from his readers and acquaintances in Little Rock. "They'd tell me, 'Say, I really like that website of yours, and you know, I used to buy the paper but I don't need to anymore.'" Of course, he recalled, "we were all waiting for the digital-advertising bonanza that was going to make all the difference." But it never came, so in 2001, after two years, he changed his mind. No more free *Democrat-Gazette*. You could read it online, but you'd have to pay or be a print subscriber. "Between 2001 and 2011, we did not lose any circulation, while a lot of dailies were losing a third or even a half of theirs," he told me.

The paper has also maintained its news hole—the space given to editorial content—and its newsroom employment is better than many papers in similar markets. When many regional papers have reduced newsroom employees to fifty or sixty, the *Democrat-Gazette* still had 106 staffers.

Despite this relatively strong position, Hussman said, his paper lost money in 2018 for the first time in twenty-five years. He calculates that circulation that once was 180,000 daily and 220,000 on Sunday is around half that now. If Hussman's iPad idea sounds far-fetched and unlikely to succeed, that's because it is admittedly a desperate measure for a desperate time. "My dad was a fabulous businessman and he used to ask people if they'd heard about the rabbit that climbed a tree. Somebody would say, well, rabbits don't climb trees. And he'd reply, 'I know, but this one had to.'" And so, too, he hopes for newspaper readers and their free iPads. "If I hadn't devoted forty-five years of my life to this, there is no way I would be doing this." Will this

64   rabbit be able to climb the tree? In Hussman's mind, it simply has to.

"It's really important to the public to have the watchdog," he said. The outlook is far from bright, even given Hussman's approach. And it's worse elsewhere: "I'm real pessimistic. I'm afraid that five or six years out, we're going to end up with no local newspapers. And I'll tell you what: It's going to be a field day for corruption."

East Palo Alto, California

Once served by two weeklies, the small, multi-ethnic, relatively poor city of East Palo Alto has become a news desert. The results, as surveyed by the *Washington Post*'s Paul Farhi, are depressing: There was no news coverage for a week, when 80 percent of the school district's 184 teachers, in an emotional public meeting, protested what they saw as the school superintendent's mismanagement and signed a vote of no confidence. Finally, nearby city dailies published a story or two, and then dropped the issue. And when it came time in 2016 to elect a new city council in East Palo Alto and to decide on three ballot measures, including two that would raise local taxes, there was virtually no advance coverage. The *Palo Alto Daily News* mentioned the council race just once before Election Day, Farhi reported. "The rival *Palo Alto Daily Post* listed the candidates' names in August—and then didn't report another word until after Election Day."

Lexington, Virginia

Darryl Woodson was busy, though too experienced to be frantic, on a Tuesday afternoon in October 2019, as deadline approached for the weekly *News-Gazette*. There was a big story happening: The former head nurse in the Rockbridge Regional Jail, who was convicted in a federal case involving the abuse of a prisoner, was being sentenced. The next morning, the story carried a large headline across the top of the paper's front page: "Hassler Given One Year." Page One also featured informative coverage of the candidates for the following week's Board of Supervisors elections and some other meaty political news.

Woodson, a wiry man who, despite his graying hair, looks too young to have been at the paper since 1983, found a few minutes amid the news rush to tell me that he's worried. Advertising revenue is way down at the *News-Gazette* from the days when there were three car dealerships in the area eager to take out full-page ads on a regular basis. And he's thought about whether it would make sense to reduce expenses by trimming his editorial staff, even though he makes do now with only two-and-a-half reporting positions. The whole newspaper operation, including the advertising and circulation staff, amounts to thirteen employees; the broadsheet, with its crisp color photographs, is printed in Lynchburg at the daily *News & Advance*, about an hour southeast.

"We're getting by, but it's really gotten tough," he said. The paper has tried to find new sources of revenue. The monthly, free-standing real estate section, heavy with ads, is helping to stanch the bleeding. The newspaper itself carries slick circulars from Walmart, Kroger's supermarket, CVS, and other chain advertisers. But it's a far cry from the old days.

If this family-owned newspaper were to fail, like so many other small weeklies in the United States, Lexington's quality of life would suffer, residents were quick to tell me. "We've only got the *News-Gazette* and one radio station, so other than that, there's just social media," said a clerk at The Georges, a boutique hotel, where an array of the day's printed newspapers are laid out for the guests: the *Washington Post*, the *New York Times*, the *Wall Street Journal*, *USA Today*, and the *Richmond Times-Dispatch*. This small town is dominated by Washington & Lee University, and student journalists produce a weekly website and broadcast called the Rockbridge Report that provides regional coverage. If the *News-Gazette* were to fail, Lexington would become yet another town too dependent on student publications for news. "When the Student Newspaper Is the Only Daily Paper in Town," goes a *New York Times* headline in 2019 chronicling the problems facing Ann Arbor, Michigan.

In the fall of 2018, President Trump's then-press secretary, Sarah Sanders, was asked to leave a tiny farm-to-table restaurant in Lexington, the Red Hen. Owner Stephanie Wilkinson made the decision not to serve Sanders and her party after conferring with her staff—they were in agreement that some of the Trump administration's decisions and actions were so offensive that one of his chief representatives simply wasn't welcome. After much ado on Twitter, the event became a flashpoint for the polarized politics of the nation—and of the region. The *News-Gazette* covered the Red Hen contretemps with news stories and commentary, but Woodson made the decision to publish every local letter-to-the-editor that he received, as long as they met certain editorial standards. That resulted in pages and pages of passionately expressed missives printed over several weeks. "We might have published a hundred letters. I kind of lost count," Woodson said, as we stood in the front office of the paper's one-story brick building located in the heart of small-town Lexington: a town that features the Stone-wall Jackson House and Museum, and where Robert E. Lee, the onetime university president and Confederate commander, is buried under the campus chapel that bears his name. The region and the university have grappled with conflicting ideas about their history, at times focusing on Confederate flags and monuments. There was even a proposal to change the name of the university, although, as one student journalist told me with utter conviction, "That will never, never happen." Lexington may be small, but it's not without news.

Global Problems

The Roman Catholic Church is the largest international organization in the world, overseeing some 1.3 billion worshippers on every continent in practically every country on the globe. So when a group of foreign correspondents and international journalists gathered at the Vatican in September 2019 to meet Pope Francis, they might have been a little surprised to hear the worldwide head of half a million clergy confess that what was on his mind was local news. "It is the most genuine and the most authentic in the mass-media world," he said, and citizens of all countries need "to intercept the same reality, to be able to transmit to a wider horizon all those values that belong to the life and history of the people, and at the same time give voice to poverty, challenges, sometimes urgent issues in the territories, along the streets, meeting families, in places of work." Its immersion in "the daily, local reality, made up of people, events, projects, problems and hopes" is what makes it so important, and he implored reporters to do a better job covering news on the local level.

Unsurprisingly, the newspaper business is also declining all over Europe. Anna Masera, the ombudswoman for *LaStampa*, a daily newspaper published in Turin, told me that, in Italy, print circulation has plummeted from 2.4 million daily in 2008 to less than a million in 2019. But, other than Pope Francis, "hardly anybody in Italy talks about this local news crisis," Masera told me. "They all struggle on their own." Small digital sites are cropping up, but "these newsrooms are tiny, and the staff and collaborators underpaid, and they mostly rewrite press releases." The result is a less informed public, at a time when Italian politics is especially tumultuous. Not only did its government collapse in 2019, but the cash-strapped country was also the European country hit hardest by the coronavirus pandemic.

In conversation after conversation with journalists worldwide, I heard a similar story. Flavia Lima, the ombudswoman for *Folha*, one of the largest and most influential news organizations in Brazil, said that smaller papers and other news outlets are struggling with the same problems that American papers are having. A study found that 64 million Brazilians, almost a third of the population, live in news deserts or near deserts. All over the country, eighty-one news organizations have closed since 2011.

Angela Pimenta, director of the Institute for the Development of Journalism, or Projor—"an NGO that could be compared to a Poynter Institute wannabe," as she put it—has been involved in mapping news outlets, both print and broadcast, within 5,570 municipalities, for the resulting research project, Atlas da Notícia. In a country of 208 million inhabitants, the ten leading newspapers garner only 1.44 million subscribers, including print and digital, she said.

She named three overarching factors: the economic crisis in Brazil, digital disruption, and demographics. Adding to this is a new worry: President Jair Bolsonaro's administration no longer requires government agencies to publish public notices in Brazil's print newspapers, thus cutting into a steady revenue source. Brazil's National Association of Newspapers called it "another government initiative to weaken journalistic activity by hitting newspapers financially." It is especially hard, the organization said, "on small and medium newspapers in the interior of the country, where the so-called news deserts are already forming." Bolsonaro, a far-right nationalist elected in 2018, has attacked news organizations and criticized coverage in a technique that should be familiar to observers of President Trump. The two have praised each other, and Trump has expressed approval of Bolsonaro's use of the expression "fake news" to slam the press. In all, Pimenta said, there are serious concerns about the ability of the Brazilian press to hold government accountable, and the remote regions of the vast country have the worst of it.

In Australia, Chris Janz, the managing director of a major news conglomerate, announced in 2017 that two dominant legacy newspapers in the country—the *Age*, based in Melbourne, and the *Sydney Morning Herald*—would make big job cutbacks, perhaps as many as 120 editorial positions. The parent company, Australian Metro Publishing, sought to save $30 million as revenue fell. Janz's words sounded all too familiar to those who follow the news industry in America and around the world: "Like all publishers globally, we are confronting challenges. Print circulation and revenue have declined. While our digital audience is vastly bigger, digital revenue is less certain in the face of mega players Facebook and Google."

In Portugal, Catarina Carvalho, the executive director of *Diario de Noticias*, a daily newspaper in Lisbon, told me: "The Portuguese local media have never been very important. It's a matter of scale. The country is so tiny [11 million at best] that there is no critical mass for a strong local press. There are many media, but few sustainable. Most of them have always been very dependent, either on the Church or the local governments . . . for support and financing. Now we are seeing a new trend: Evangelical religions are buying local radios."

The United States' neighbor to the north is experiencing similar troubles, the executive director of the Canadian Journalism Foundation, Natalie Turvey, told me. With its vast open spaces and regions that are sparsely populated, Canada may be particularly susceptible to having regions beset by news poverty.

But the problem hits the major Canadian population centers, too. The Local News Research Project at Ryerson University in Toronto found that well over two hundred newspapers (mostly weeklies but some dailies, too) have closed since 2008. That's roughly a fifth of the news organizations in Canada, according to April Lindgren, who heads the project. "I was fascinated by the fact that Brampton, a large suburban municipality near Toronto with nearly 700,000 people, until recently had no local radio station, no local television station, no daily newspaper, and no serious online news outlets," she said. "A new investigative online site launched recently, but until it came along, the city's residents had only one local news source, a community newspaper that publishes once per week and its companion website."

Rasmus Kleis Nielsen, director of the Reuters Institute for the Study of Journalism, told me that it's hard to judge the overall

72 state of local journalism globally. "Data is uneven and incomplete in many countries." Is the situation worse in the United States, where more than two thousand weekly and daily newspapers have folded in the past decade or so? "Local newspapers were more plentiful and profitable in the United States than in most other countries in the late twentieth century because a) a big country created geographically distinct markets and b) a big advertising spend generated lots of revenues even though print was in long-term decline."

With the move to digital, the first factor no longer matters very much for advertising. As ad money goes online, the revenue drop has become precipitous. In the few countries where local news seems to be enduring fairly well—Norway, for example—there has been a heavier dependence on "reader revenue" or subscriptions, as opposed to advertising. What's more, "local papers were more accustomed to competition from multiple national papers with genuinely national distribution, so they had to work harder to acquire and retain subscribers/attention."

While things may look worse in the United States—and may actually be worse—it's tough all over. Technology, changing demographics, and troubled finances don't discriminate on the basis of geography. Many of the same discouraging results follow when dependable news sources cut their staffs or disappear altogether: less civic engagement, more political polarization, more potential for government corruption. These are global trends, and global problems.

New Models

With his cries of "fake news" and insistence that journalists are the enemy of the American people, President Trump made his opposition to the traditional press a hallmark of his campaign and his presidency. Trust was low—by most measurements only about a third of the public had a favorable or even tolerable view of the press. But there was one bright spot: local news. Nearly half of Americans said they trust reporting by local news organizations "a great deal" or "quite a lot," a study from Gallup and the Knight Foundation showed. Yet local news is exactly what was fading, if not dying.

Efforts to help, or at least to think through the worsening problem, have intensified. Foundations poured money into nonprofit news outfits. Advocacy organizations called for legislative changes to help newspapers survive. Even Facebook and Google made efforts, though these were sometimes greeted in the journalism world with tremendous skepticism. A few even suggested direct government subsidies to support journalism.

74   There would be no perfect solution—but now, at least, the problem was front and center.

In late 2019, two of the most respected names in journalism, ProPublica and the Texas Tribune, announced that they would join forces, vastly increasing their government-accountability coverage with a new eleven-member investigative unit based in the Tribune's Austin newsroom. The journalism produced, funded with a large gift from Houston-based Arnold Ventures, would be published on both organizations' platforms. Pro-Publica, probably the best known and most acclaimed of the digital news sites, was founded in 2007, largely through the philanthropy of San Francisco billionaires Herbert and Marion Sandler. Its journalism excelled and was repeatedly recognized at the highest levels. Remarkably, from 2009 to 2019, it won five Pulitzer Prizes. The Texas Tribune, founded in 2009, was the largest and one of the best of the local nonprofit news organizations, one that already had a hefty staff and well-established funding sources. The pairing of these two big players was enough to provide at least some hope. But how can this be reproduced in every community of the nation?

John Thornton is a wealthy investor who could be doing just about anything with his time and money. What he has chosen to do is found something called the American Journalism Project, which seeks "to reinvigorate local news through the power of venture philanthropy." His partner and co-founder in the effort is Elizabeth Green, who a few years earlier had helped start a successful education-news site, Chalkbeat.

The first step was to raise money—$50 million, "enough to make a difference, to provoke the boldness this moment in history requires, but not so much that we couldn't invest it responsibly," Green explained. Then they would invest the money in civic news organizations, defined as "a local news organization distinguished by its public service mission and commitment to meeting the critical information needs of the community—in areas such as government, environment, education, social and criminal justice, or public health."

Thornton, like Green, had some impressive successes to back up what otherwise might have seemed like a pipe dream. Thornton and his wife, Julie, provided $1 million to get the Texas Tribune started in 2009. The Tribune wasn't the first of these kinds of local sites: MinnPost and Voice of San Diego had already been established in Minnesota and California. But it quickly became a dominant player. One of Thornton's two co-founders was Evan Smith, who brought an entrepreneurial spirit and apparently endless energy to the task of finding ways for the Tribune to support itself. On-site advertising was not the answer, but running journalism-related events turned out to be a major factor. The most prominent example was the Texas Tribune Festival in Austin, several days in the early fall in which sponsors, media partners, working journalists, students, and celebrities get together to talk, learn, and party.

As I traveled to Austin for the 2019 festival, my flight from New York City carried presidential candidate Amy Klobuchar, former CBS news anchor Dan Rather, and former Department of Homeland Security secretary Jeh Johnson. A quick walk on a downtown Austin street brought glimpses of Obama administration chief strategist David Axelrod and former U.S. Ambassador to the United Nations Samantha Power. Later, onstage, Smith interviewed House Speaker Nancy Pelosi, who had just opened the impeachment inquiry into President Trump days before. The event would raise about $1 million for the Tribune's local watchdog journalism. Within a few years of the Trib's founding, the festival was attracting thousands of participants and more than a million dollars in revenue.

As Heidi Legg, director of special projects at Harvard's Shorenstein Center on Media, Politics, and Public Policy, wrote: "Two revenue paths have diverged in local news: donations or digital subscriptions. As a result, we see for-profits like the major dailies and national magazines doubling down on transforming into digital juggernauts that can compete on those platforms in delivery and win back subscribers. We also see upstarts and legacies converting into a nonprofit for public good where donors keep the newsroom afloat."

For local newspapers, the digital-subscription route has been a difficult path. Big papers like the *Washington Post* and the *New York Times* can draw from a national or perhaps even a global audience. The local papers cannot. While subscription revenue must be a major part of the answer, it is not clear that it can be the main savior.

The nonprofit route may be more successful. In most cases, nonprofits are not legacy operations with legacy costs, such as printing presses, fleets of trucks, and salaries for unionized employees that reflect what was possible in more profitable days. They are nimbler, often digital-only, or certainly digital-first, with an occasional or weekly print product.

In Buffalo, there's Investigative Post, a small but impressive news organization that concentrates on holding public officials accountable. A former *Buffalo News* investigative reporter, James Heaney, started it from scratch not long after he took a

buyout from his longtime newspaper job. At the *News*, he was a
longtime leader of the local chapter of the Newspaper Guild and
his dogged reporting had won awards and other recognition.

When Heaney and I worked in the same newsroom, we
sometimes disagreed vehemently, despite our mutual respect.
His point of view was that "all good work is done in defiance
of management." I was management. Once we no longer shared
the fraught atmosphere of the same newsroom, we became
better friends, and I've watched as he and his small staff have
forged a new way of reporting in the Buffalo area. Most notably,
Investigative Post reported on New York State's request for
proposals for the construction of projects that were part of
Governor Andrew Cuomo's "Buffalo Billion" effort intended
to direct a billion dollars to shoring up the region's troubled
post-industrial economy. Heaney's reporting revealed that the
requests were tailored to favor one local developer, a major campaign contributor to Cuomo. Building on the reporting, Preet
Bharara, then the U.S. Attorney for the Southern District of
New York, began an investigation that eventually resulted in
the conviction of several state officials and campaign contribu-
tors on corruption charges, and a legislative effort to reform the
state's practices for awarding contracts. Investigative Post also
reported on improper Buffalo police practices that unfairly targeted minority residents; the unit at the heart of the abuses has
since been disbanded.

That's impressive work for a tiny shop like Investigative
Post, a place where Heaney does much of the development work
as well as the journalism, and has had some anxious moments
about his organization's finances. Like other local nonprofit
newsrooms, Investigative Post has partnerships with more

established media organizations, particularly with one of the local television stations, WGRZ-TV, and with WBFO, the local public radio station. On occasion, their work has even appeared in the *Buffalo News*. As of 2019, Buffalo is still quite fortunate in terms of watchdog journalism, despite being one of the poorest cities in the United States. Investigative journalism is working at the moment in Buffalo, but it's every bit as tenuous as the entire national media landscape. There's no guarantee that any of it will be around in five years. The old business model is broken for good; the present and future must be created anew, and on the run.

Nonprofit newsrooms like Puerto Rico's Center for Investigative Journalism (known as CPI) published documents in the summer of 2019 that brought down the territory's governor, Ricardo A. Rossello. The CPI was just a decade or so old, and then only employing ten full-time reporters and editors; it specializes in obtaining otherwise unavailable material, often through lawsuits. The CPI obtained nearly nine hundred pages of chat messages between Rossello and his male cronies, many of them misogynistic, homophobic, and dismissive. The messages, along with CPI's accompanying investigative stories about corruption, so infuriated the populace that hundreds of thousands of Puerto Ricans took to the streets to demand the governor's ouster. With impeachment looming, he had no choice but to step down. A small nonprofit enterprise had gone far beyond what traditional newspapers in Puerto Rico had produced. Independent, scrappy, and nimble, the CPI was funded mostly by donations, which are not always easy to come by. Unprecedented amounts of financial support flowed to the CPI after their remarkable reporting triumph. It didn't hurt that even theater superstar Lin-Manuel Miranda tweeted to his worldwide audience, urging support.

But funding for nonprofit journalism can be a constant, gnawing problem for those who run them. Richard Tofel, president of ProPublica, said that one of the biggest problems is that no matter how much the nonprofit journalism sector grows, it's unlikely to replace a thriving newspaper in every good-sized town in America. "Nothing scales like capitalism, and non-profits don't naturally replicate themselves," he told me. Non-profits "have to be scaled artisanally," in small batches.

Donors—whether individual philanthropists, foundations, or even news consumers—can be fickle and difficult to please. They may want some kind of editorial control or at least ability to direct the focus of the work. "Donors want to achieve what they want to achieve," Tofel said. "If you are dealing with people of integrity and goodwill, it's not a huge problem." After all, advertisers have been known to express their displeasure with a negative story by withdrawing their advertising dollars. But one angry car dealer was not a big loss when there were dozens of other advertisers available to soften the blow. In a nonprofit that's dependent on just a few big donors, their unhappiness can really hurt. There are ways to deal with this, like establishing guidelines about editorial independence up front, but, as American Press Institute executive director Tom Rosenstiel pointed out, very few nonprofits have such guidelines. "There is no such thing as revenue that comes without risk," Rosenstiel said.

Businesses are accustomed to competing with others in their regions, but now it's become crucially important for journalism outfits to cooperate. In Pennsylvania, a group of journalists and news organizations, including the *Philadelphia*

80   *Inquirer* and the *Pittsburgh Post-Gazette*, have come together to form Spotlight PA, which employs eight reporters who focus strictly on state politics. Eight might seem like a small number, but in fact Spotlight PA has the largest newsroom in Pennsylvania dedicated solely to covering state government. A Pew Research study in 2014 found that the number of full-time statehouse reporters around the country had dropped by 35 percent since 2003, and this was before some of the most serious retrenchment.

Nonprofits and other digital-only startups are not the only way forward for local news. Heidi Legg, in her Shorenstein Center research, identifies several other trends that may prove fruitful. One is what she calls "the Billionaire Local Newspaper Club," in which wealthy investors, usually members of the community, put "massive infusions of capital" into local newspapers so that they "can get up to speed digitally." Most notably, perhaps, this has happened at the *Los Angeles Times*. Long one of the nation's best and most prominent regional news organizations, it fell on hard times in recent years as its parent company, then named Tronc (formerly and currently named Tribune Publishing), insisted on deep staff cuts and sent in one top editor after another to make changes. In early 2018, billionaire biotech investor Patrick Soon-Shiong came forward to buy the paper. Since then, the *Times*, under editor Norman Pearlstine, has restored its reputation. It is hiring top talent from around the country, and working on its financial stability.

Like the purchase of the *Washington Post* by Amazon founder Jeff Bezos several years earlier, this radical turn of events offers to give the *Los Angeles Times* what Bezos called "runway"—enough time and money to gain momentum, to stabilize, and to figure things out. That has worked extremely well for the *Post,* which describes itself now as profitable, in part because it redefined its audience as national, even global—no longer as mostly regional. With print advertising so diminished, and digital advertising going mostly to the big-tech platforms, success in garnering large numbers of digital subscriptions is an absolute necessity. Early difficulties in doing so resulted in some dire headlines, but that began to turn around in 2020, even before the pandemic hit and made its journalism even more essential. The *Boston Globe* has been relatively successful on this front, moving aggressively to incentivize its readers to become digital subscribers. Locally owned papers like the *Post and Courier* in Charleston, South Carolina, have managed to combine quality journalism and economic stability through forging close connections with subscribers.

Not every community has a Soon-Siong or a Bezos. In fact, this model remains a rarity. It is certainly not something that can be counted on to save the day across the country. There's no law that says every billionaire will make a good owner, or that the very rich have any particular talent for the role. Consider what's happened in Las Vegas, where casino tycoon Sheldon Adelson has bought the *Review-Journal,* a paper that previously had a strong reputation for tough reporting, particularly in holding the casino industry to account. Adelson soon started exerting influence on the coverage. A former ranking editor, James Wright, disclosed that, on orders from above, the paper provided "boosterish" coverage of Adelson's efforts to move the Oakland Raiders to Las Vegas. There were "glowing stories" about new restaurants at Adelson's properties, "lapdog coverage" of federal investigations of his business practices, a "sudden elevation" of reporting on the basketball team at a school supported by the Adelsons, and "hyper-coverage" of the opening of the Sands's new Macau property, which included flying staff to China. "It's not like paper owners haven't done things like this in the past," Wright said. "But with Adelson, it's on steroids."

By contrast, Jeff Bezos has not attempted to influence coverage at the *Washington Post*. And in my experience over many years, Warren Buffett never called a single editorial shot at the *Buffalo News*.

Surveying other possible approaches to local news, Heidi Legg identified "mobilizers" and "accelerators." Mobilizers, like the American Journalism Project, bolster local newsrooms with external support and staff. Another example is Report for America, which funds the addition of young journalists into existing newsrooms, for a limited time. It's a national service project, an effort that has been compared to the Peace Corps. The first class of Report for America journalists entered newsrooms in 2018, with funding from some familiar names: the Google News Initiative, the Knight Foundation, and Craig Newmark, among others. By 2020, the project had grown significantly, so that hundreds of young reporters were being dispatched throughout the United States.

Accelerators borrow their concepts from the startup model in the tech world, training journalists in growing and using digital tools. Included in this category are the Information Accelerator, the Lenfest Institute, Facebook Accelerator, Google News Initiative, and the Membership Puzzle at NYU.

Not all of these, though, have been entirely well received in the journalism community. Plenty of people think that Facebook's and Google's efforts to help local news are disingenuous or, at least, insufficient. After wrecking the business model, to their great financial advantage, they are essentially throwing their sofa change at the problem. In late 2019, Facebook announced that it would start paying publishers for their journalism. Some heralded the "Facebook News Tab" as an important step forward. But for the most part, it helps those publishers who are already on the road to survival: the *New York Times*, the *Washington Post*, Bloomberg News, BuzzFeed News, and others. A few of the largest metro news organizations, including, for example, the *Philadelphia Inquirer*, will benefit. But the vast majority of local papers, especially those in heartland America, won't see a dime. It's hardly encouraging that Breitbart News, a platform for right-leaning propaganda and white-supremacist views rather than a legitimate news organization, was considered one of Facebook News's "trusted sources."

Another Facebook local-journalism effort, the Community Network, was expected to get about $1.5 million in funding in 2019—less than 1 percent of the company's revenue in a day. Facebook's broader Journalism Project is expected to receive $300 million in the next few years, about two days' worth of the company's revenue.

These efforts do show that the local-news crisis is increasingly getting more attention. The questions, though, are pressing ones: Will it be too late? Are any of them capable of making a major difference? One organization that is fighting a related battle is the News Media Alliance, which represents publishers. It was once known as the Newspaper Association of America; its name change—like that of the once-mighty American Society of Newspaper Editors, now the News Leaders Association—is just one more sign of the flagging influence of newspapers nationwide. In 2019, the News Media Alliance was throwing its weight behind a bill in both houses of Congress, one with bipartisan support, that would allow publishers to negotiate together with Facebook and Google. That would require a temporary anti-trust exemption, a so-called "safe harbor" for a four-year period, while the publishers would try to right their capsizing ships.

Would such an exemption really shore up newspapers' flagging finances? David Chavern, chief executive of the News Media Alliance, wrote a widely circulated op-ed piece making the case that it would. Google and Facebook have profited immensely from the content supplied by publishers, he wrote, quoting a study that said Google made an estimated $4.7 billion in revenue from news content in 2018. Little of that came to the sources of the content. "While information may want to be free, journalists need to get paid," Chavern wrote. "This requires finding common rules for a fair and equitable online ecosystem that allows publishers to maintain the quality of their content that readers expect." A temporary "safe harbor" from anti-trust rules might be an important step in that direction, but as with all such measures involving local news, positive change comes haltingly with uncertain results, while the negative trends— the loss of newsroom jobs and the revenue that sustains them— continue at a breakneck pace.

Nicholas Lemann, dean emeritus of the Columbia University Graduate School of Journalism, and director of Columbia

Global Reports (the publisher of this book), gives serious consideration to an idea to support public-interest reporting that
journalists have traditionally run screaming from: direct government subsidy. "Almost all American journalists react to this
idea with a strong visceral recoil, especially now," Lemann wrote.

> But the severity of the situation demands subjecting our
> automatic assumptions to more careful scrutiny. Govern-
> ment support can be structured in many different ways; great
> portions of the independent truth-seeking activity in the
> United States are funded by the government, reasonably suc-
> cessfully, despite enormous built-in potential for political
> interference. The Federal Reserve employs many more pro-
> fessional research economists than any economics depart-
> ment. Public libraries, almost all the time, are permitted to
> acquire their books and research materials freely. University
> research—indeed, universities generally, including private
> universities—are overwhelmingly supported by the govern-
> ment, including when their work touches on politically con-
> troversial subjects.

Lemann argues that "such government funding systems
require several layers of built-in protection from the whims
of elected officials. Usually these are peer-review mechanisms
that determine where funding goes specifically and ensure that
it cannot be cut off capriciously without warning."

It may be an idea, once almost unthinkable, whose time
has finally come. It's not unreasonable, after all, to argue that
one kind of government help—an anti-trust exemption for

86　publishers, for example—should be no more troubling to journalistic purists than direct subsidies. I'm not sure that's true, particularly in a time when the very notion of journalistic truth is under siege from political actors. We don't want the likes of Donald Trump or disgraced Buffalo-area congressman Chris Collins deciding what constitutes "fake news" because it doesn't serve their political purposes of the moment.

Certainly such a development would require careful consideration and built-in protections. So would some of the many suggestions that bubbled up in the spring of 2020, as news organizations reeled from the coronavirus meltdown. These included doubling federal funds for public media, and $500 million in spending for public-health ads through local media. In a sweeping *Columbia Journalism Review* piece, Steve Waldman, president of Report for America, offered a range of other ideas, including legislative and regulatory changes. Among them: adopting anti-trust and tax laws that would limit consolidation and "financialization" of local news; making it easier for commercial news organizations to convert into nonprofit entities, as the *Salt Lake Tribune* did in 2019; and enforcing the FCC's "public interest obligation" for local commercial TV stations, with an emphasis on requiring local reporting.

I'm interested in anything reasonable that will help local journalism stay alive. As PEN America's "Losing the News" study puts it, "a radical rethinking of local journalism as a public good" has become necessary. The report calls for the formation of a new congressional commission to "develop concrete recommendations for how the government can better support a free and independent local press." I'm not persuaded that direct

government subsidies to news organizations are a good idea
but I also don't rule them out. As with so many aspects of the
local-journalism crisis, old ideas on this subject—however well
founded and well accepted in an earlier era—should be subject
to reexamination.

Conclusion

A decade ago, Clay Shirky, one of the most insightful thinkers on the internet's effects on journalism, surveyed all the panicky things newspaper executives were considering to save their industry, including lawsuits against content-stealers, poorly conceived paywalls, and systems of "micro payments" to news organizations for individual articles. His essay "Newspapers and Thinking the Unthinkable" has since become a seminal piece of writing for being sharply critical of those who were steadfastly denying what he saw as the obvious endgame.

When reality is labeled unthinkable, it creates a kind of sickness in an industry. Leadership becomes faith-based, while employees who have the temerity to suggest that what seems to be happening is in fact happening are herded into Innovation Departments, where they can be ignored en bloc. This shunting aside of the realists in favor of the fabulists has different effects on different industries at different times. One of the effects on the newspapers is that many of their most passionate defenders are unable, even now, to plan for a world in which the industry they knew is visibly going away. . . .

Round and round this goes, with the people committed to saving newspapers demanding to know "If the old model is broken, what will work in its place?" To which the answer is: nothing. Nothing will work. There is no general model for newspapers to replace the one the Internet just broke.

The newspaper industry now comprises two distinct groups: the haves and the have-nots. National giants like the *New York Times,* the *Wall Street Journal,* and the *Washington Post* belong to the former, largely through convincing millions of readers to pay for digital subscriptions. With very few exceptions, local newspapers fall into the second category. Many are becoming "toast," in Warren Buffett's all-too-memorable phrase.

But the journalism remains vital. Local newspapers like the *Palm Beach Post* and the *Miami Herald* have for years doggedly told the unsavory story of sex trafficker Jeffrey Epstein, who would eventually face federal charges and then die in prison. *Herald* reporter Julie K. Brown's decision to interview the girls and women that Epstein victimized was what made all the difference, and she did this work after many thought that the Epstein saga had gone stale. What happens when there isn't a news organization that can give a reporter the time and resources for such work? One that has lawyers on staff or on call? Editors with serious investigative experience? The story may be known to some, but never fully revealed. In the Epstein case, the federal prosecutor charging him acknowledged that his team had been "assisted by some excellent investigative journalism."

By late 2019, major Rust Belt papers were suffering particularly tough blows. The *Pittsburgh Post-Gazette*, which won a Pulitzer Prize for its coverage of the Tree of Life synagogue massacre in 2018, was swiftly reducing the number of days the paper would be available in print for home delivery. Joshua Benton of Nieman Lab tallied up the medium-to-large cities in the region that no longer have a seven-day home-delivered print newspaper: Pittsburgh, Youngstown, Cleveland, Detroit, Ann Arbor, Flint, Grand Rapids, Syracuse, Harrisburg, Toledo. Many of these cities are poor—in fact, some of the poorest in the nation. This fact, no doubt, contributes to the newspapers' financial problems; their advertising markets are likely to be limited and weak, and they may have communities that are less digitally oriented, so less likely to buy digital subscriptions. Home delivery of a printed paper certainly isn't the most dependable measure of a news organization's value, but when it withers away, something important is lost.

New, all-digital news sites, many of them nonprofits, are essential. But, according to one significant study, they are not yet as important as newspaper companies, even in the shrunken and faded state that newspapers are in. Two researchers at Duke University, Philip Napoli and Jessica Mahone, studied a hundred communities across the United States to explore which types of outlets are the most significant producers of journalism. They analyzed more than 16,000 stories to determine whether each met the following criteria: Was the story local? Was it original? Did it address a critical information need? The results should give pause to those ready to say this legacy medium is a thing of the past: Newspapers produce more local reporting than television, radio, and online-only outlets combined. "There needs

92   to be more of a focus on how do you support newspapers best," Mahone told me. "That doesn't reflect how a lot of philanthropies are approaching the problem." Philanthropists and foundations tend to pour money into startups and nonprofits, while newspapers often are considered something to leave behind as quickly as possible. One well-intentioned journalism advocate wrote off newspapers by saying that "the ship has sailed." "The idea that we have a news ecosystem ready to replace newspapers is just false," Mahone said.

What worries Joel Berg most about the decline of local journalism is that poor people and advocates for the disenfranchised have far fewer ways to get their message out. The rich and powerful, on the other hand, always have a bully pulpit. When Berg first joined what's now known as Hunger Free America, a nonprofit based in New York City, it was called the NYC Coalition Against Hunger. "Having little money or staff, our single most effective tool to hold the City and State of New York accountable on hunger and poverty was using the local media to highlight our cause," he said. They put out press releases and held events to point to the level of hunger and poverty in New York, and to criticize government policies on food stamps, low wages, the rate of participation in free school breakfast programs, and the like. "Because we were able to get some lower-level elected officials media coverage, subsequently, high-level elected officials joined with us."

Even in a media mecca like New York City, that has changed dramatically in the past two decades, he said. "At key City Council hearings, there used to always be at least one or two local reporters present." Now, he says, such hearings sometimes have "zero press" in attendance and it's much harder to get local media coverage for his causes. (In 2019, the arrival of a new non-profit newsroom, The City, was a most welcome addition to the local-media landscape in New York's five boroughs.)

Stories about poverty and hunger are not the kind of content that gets a lot of clicks. It's not that such stories or projects can't be made compelling. As *New York Times* public editor, I examined the coverage of poverty and economic inequality issues by the *Times*. I found it of high quality but insufficient in volume, and dwarfed by stories meant to appeal to the rich, or at least those aspiring to be so. The column hit a nerve. I rarely had more reader response, most of it calling for more attention to poverty or criticizing the glitzy stories about apartments that only the 1 percent could ever hope to afford.

"The fates of communities and local news organizations are intrinsically linked," UNC's Penny Abernathy said in a 2018 talk. Strong local papers have "encouraged social cohesion and political activism." That may seem theoretical, but it's all very real once it starts to fade away. When I visited Luzerne County in northeastern Pennsylvania to talk to people about their media habits, I was struck by the attitudes about local news outlets. The county was one of those critical places that had voted for President Obama in 2008 and 2012, and flipped red to Trump in 2016. The most reasonable people I talked to, no matter whom they had voted for, were regular readers of the local papers and regular watchers of the local news. Among all news sources, it is local news that manages to maintain at least some trust even in this deeply polarized political environment. The trust in local news is breaking down, but not as badly as trust in national news, according to a Gallup/Knight poll.

94   To those who argue that many of the functions of newspapers are outdated—you can get the weather report and movie times elsewhere and more efficiently—I would point out that it's not just the watchdog journalism that matters. It's the way a local columnist can express a community's frustration or triumph, the way the local music critic can review a concert, the deeply reported feature stories, the assessment of a new restaurant, the obituaries, the letters to the editor. The newspaper ties a region together, helps it make sense of itself, fosters a sense of community, serves as a village square whose boundaries transcend Facebook's filter bubble.

     Barbara O'Brien, the *Buffalo News* reporter who scrutinized the troubling town finances in Orchard Park, is still on the job. (After her reporting about the mysterious $100,000 payout to the police chief, a town board member published an apologetic open letter to residents: "We failed in this circumstance, and we are indebted to the media and many citizens for holding our feet to the fire.") the *Buffalo News* is still being delivered to households, and its coronavirus coverage, provided for free online, served its community well. But painful pay reductions and staff furloughs soon followed 2020's economic downturn, as they did at so many news organizations worldwide. The four television stations in town are doing some enterprise reporting, and the local nonprofit, Investigative Post, has expanded its staff. Journalism is still happening in my hometown. Many communities aren't nearly as fortunate.

My research for this book, combined with my decades in journalism, has left me with a great deal of sadness about what is happening and what is to come in the next several years. But

I'm certainly not without hope. The loss of local news will continue, especially in the rural or remote areas that the newer efforts are unlikely to reach. The damage done by those losses will accelerate. American politics will become even more polarized; government and business corruption will flourish; the glue that holds communities together will weaken.

And though there is no stopping this momentum, I am convinced that those who care about good journalism have to do whatever is possible to make things better—more than is being done now. We must shore up newspapers with thoughtful policy changes. We must support existing news organizations and keep them operating as long as possible. We must encourage and sustain the new efforts that are filling at least some of the gaping holes, and are becoming more important every day.

I think of the words of Antonio Gramsci, the Italian political writer jailed by Mussolini's Fascist regime, who advocated what he called "pessimism of the intellect and optimism of the will." If you know that your wood-frame house is on fire and the nearest fire department is many miles away, you still have to call 911, get out your garden hose and bucket, and keep acting as if the fire trucks are on the way.

So, too, with local news. The match was struck years ago, the kerosene poured, and the house is very much ablaze. But for the sake of democracy, in America and around the world, we need to save as much as possible of what remains, bringing the traditional strengths fully into the digital age. And, at the same time, we must energetically support and foster the newer models that are forging the local journalism so necessary for today and tomorrow.

I appreciate those experts whose work I have drawn on or who generously provided information and guidance: Penny Muse Abernathy, Joshua Benton, Ken Doctor, Rasmus Kleis Nielsen, Tom Rosenstiel, Heidi Legg, Anna Masera, and others. Many thanks to my early readers to whom I turned with apprehension: Sophie Kleeman, Brian Connolly, Matt Wolfson, and Richard Tofel. Thanks, too, to Jo Constantz for her painstaking help with endnotes. I am grateful to my editors at the *Washington Post*, who supported this effort and allowed me the time to get it done, particularly Marty Baron, Tracy Grant, Liz Seymour, and David Malitz; and to the small but powerhouse team at Columbia Global Reports: Nicholas Lemann, Camille McDuffie, and Jimmy So. Finally, I want to honor my former colleagues at the *Buffalo News*, some of whom are still working there amid all the difficulties of this moment. Their talent, heart, and dedication inspire me, as does the work of local journalists all over the world.

Democracy's Detectives: The Economics of Investigative Journalism,
James T. Hamilton

Hamilton, a Stanford University professor, explains how high-quality
journalism helps to hold government and businesses accountable. His
impressive study, which won the prestigious Goldsmith Award, delves into
the positive effect that investigative journalism can have for citizens and
consumers, and describes how time-consuming and expensive such work
is—an especially important consideration when journalism's business
model is changing so rapidly.

"The Expanding News Desert," Penny Muse Abernathy

Abernathy is the leading academic expert on "news deserts," those regions
that have no substantial source of local news. A former executive at the
Wall Street Journal and the *New York Times,* she specializes in digital media
economics at the University of North Carolina. Her 2018 report is essential
to understanding the new ecosystem of news as it documents in detail the
decline and loss of local news organizations around the United States.

Breaking News: The Remaking of Journalism and Why It Matters Now,
Alan Rusbridger

Few journalists have had as successful or consequential a career as has
Rusbridger, the longtime top editor of Britain's *Guardian* newspaper. Not
only did he lead the transformation of the paper into a digital powerhouse
with worldwide influence; he was at the helm when his paper exposed
the phone hacking scandal by Rupert Murdoch's New International, and
worked with Edward Snowden to reveal the National Security Agency's
global surveillance system in 2013. The way journalism works now is
contained here.

"Losing the News: The Decimation of Local News and the Search for
Solutions," PEN America

This report, directed by the staff of the prominent free-expression
organization, features case studies of journalism in decline, written by
journalists based in North Carolina, Michigan, and Colorado. They show
how the loss of local news outlets has led to lower levels of government

accountability, high potential for corruption, and less public awareness of important regional issues. The report calls for a new infusion of public funding and increased philanthropic support for local journalism.

Democracy Without Journalism?: Confronting the Misinformation Society, Victor Pickard

This University of Pennsylvania professor calls for a reinvention of journalism in order to deal with underlying structural problems, not only in the business model of news but in the ways false information is spread in the social-media era. Using the election of Donald Trump as a way to examine these issues, Pickard places the current journalism crisis in historical perspective.

NOTES

INTRODUCTION

13 Barbara O'Brien: Barbara O'Brien, "Orchard Park Police Chief Gets Another $100,000 to Retire," *Buffalo News*, May 25, 2019.

15 As local journalism declines: "Losing the News," PEN America, November 20, 2019.

16 It's painful: Margaret Sullivan, "Is This Strip-mining or Journalism? 'Sobs, Gasps, Expletives' over Latest Denver Post Layoffs," *Washington Post*, March 15, 2018.

17 They're going to disappear: Sam Ro, "Warren Buffett Says the Newspaper Business Is 'Toast,'" Yahoo Finance, April 29, 2019.

17 From 2004 to 2015: Bill Reader, "Despite Losses, Community Newspapers Still Dominate the U.S. Market," *Newspaper Research Journal* 39 (2018): 32.

17 "I think most local newspapers": Joe Concha, "NYT Editor Predicts Most Local Newspapers Will 'Die in the Next Five Years,'" the *Hill*, May 22, 2019.

18 A Pew study in 2019: "For Local News, Americans Embrace Digital but Still Want Strong Community Connection," Pew Research Center: Journalism & Media, March 26, 2019.

19 A Northern California man: Margaret Sullivan, "Cancel in Protest? Or Stay with a Local Newspaper That's Being Strip-mined for Profits?" *Washington Post*, January 27, 2019.

21 a "news desert": Penelope Muse Abernathy, "The Expanding News Desert," University of North Carolina Hussman School of Journalism and Media, 2018.

22 A *Journal of Politics* study: Danny Hayes and Jennifer Lawless, "The Decline of Local News and its Effects: New Evidence from Longitudinal Data," *Journal of Politics* 80 (2017): 332.

22 Voting becomes more politically polarized: Joshua Darr, Matthew Hitt, and Johanna Dunaway, "Newspaper Closures Polarize Voting Behavior," *Journal of Communication* 68 (2018): 1007.

22 When local reporting waned: Pengjie Gao, Chang Joo Lee, and Dermot Murphy, "Financing Dies in Darkness? The Impact of Newspaper Closures on Public Finance," Brookings, September 24, 2018.

23 The harm is not confined: Yukihiro Yazaki, "Newspapers and Political Accountability: Evidence from Japan," *Public Choice* 172 (2017): 311.

23 Studies in Japan and Switzerland: Daniel Kübler and Christopher Goodman,

102   "Newspaper Markets and
Municipal Politics: How Audience
and Congruence Increase Turnout
in Local Elections," *Journal of
Elections, Public Opinion and Parties*
29 (2019): 1.

CHAPTER TWO

36   **David Gottesman:** Jonathan
Laing, "The Collector," *Wall Street
Journal*, March 31, 1977.

37   **By 2006, according to *Forbes*:**
Louis Hau, "Newspaper Killer,"
Forbes, December 11, 2006.

38   **Emily Bell:** Emily Bell, "Media
Amnesia and the Facebook News
Tab," *Columbia Journalism Review*,
October 25, 2019.

39   **As the Reuters Institute
study succinctly put it:** Joy Jenkins
and Rasmus Kleis Nielsen, "The
Digital Transition of Local News,"
Reuters Institute, 2018.

40   **Writing in Recode:** Kurt
Wagner, "TV and Newspapers Are
Out. Facebook and Google Are In,"
Recode, February 20, 2019.

41   **It's no exaggeration:** Felix
Richter, "Fifty Years of Growth
Wiped Out in a Decade," *Statista*,
September 17, 2012.

42   **What concerns Tingley:**
Margaret Sullivan, "The Local-
News Crisis Is Destroying What
a Divided America Desperately
Needs: Common Ground,"
Washington Post, August 5, 2018.

43   **Ken Doctor:** Ken Doctor,
"Newsonomics: It's Looking Like
Gannett Will Be Acquired by
GateHouse—Creating a Newspaper
Megachain Like the U.S. Has Never
Seen," Nieman Lab, July 18, 2019.

43   **As the unwelcome trend:**
Robert Kuttner and Hildy Zenger,
"Saving the Free Press from
Private Equity," *American Prospect*,
December 27, 2017.

44   **a young reporter, Jesse Aaron
Paul:** Margaret Sullivan, "Is This
Strip-mining or Journalism? 'Sobs,
Gasps, Expletives' Over Latest
Denver Post Layoffs."

45   **Jesse Paul:** Margaret
Sullivan, "Is This Strip-mining
or Journalism? 'Sobs, Gasps,
Expletives' Over Latest Denver Post
Layoffs."

45   **Just short of setting the
place on fire:** Joshua Benton, "The
Boston Herald's Buyer Is A vulture
Capitalist," *Boston Globe*, February
15, 2018.

46   **From a business perspective:**
"Local TV News Fact Sheet," Pew
Research Center: Journalism &
Media, June 25, 2019.

47   **Stations need market
differentiation:** Margaret Sullivan,
"The 'I-Team' Is Back—and It
Might Help Save Local TV News,"
Washington Post, August 7, 2016.

47   **A 2018 Knight Foundation
study:** "Local TV News and the

New Media Landscape," The Knight
Foundation, 2018.

CHAPTER THREE

51   **late columnist Mike Royko:**
Mike Royko, "A Truly Great
Newspaper, Why Couldn't It Make
It?" *Chicago Daily News*, March 4,
1978.

53   **"Crimetown, USA":** David
Grann, "Crimetown USA," *New
Republic*, July 10, 2000.

54   **decided to fund one
investigative journalist:**
"ProPublica is Expanding Its Local
Reporting Network to Youngstown,
Ohio," ProPublica, July 8, 2019.

56   **Alice Dreger:** David Dobbs,
"'Galileo's Middle Finger,' by Alice
Dreger," *New York Times*, April 17,
2015

60   **Advertisers aren't off limits:**
"Breaking: A Local Newspaper
Chain That's Actually Making Good
Money," *Forbes*, January 21, 2013.

62   **$12 million worth of free
iPads:** Kyle Massey, "Interview:
Walter Hussman on the Future of
Arkansas Newspapers," *Arkansas
Business*, May 27, 2019.

64   **80 percent of the school
district's 184 teachers:** Paul Farhi,
"What happens to local news when
there is no local media to cover it?"
Washington Post, July 17, 2017.

CHAPTER FOUR

68   **Vatican in September 2019:**
"Audience with a Delegation of
the Regional Journalism Group of
the RAI," Holy See Press Office,
September 16, 2019.

69   **Not only did its government
collapse:** Jason Horowitz, "Italy's
Government Collapses, Turning
Chaos into Crisis," *New York Times*,
August 20, 2019.

69   **A study found that 64
million Brazilians:** Alessandra
Monnerat, "Almost a Third of
Brazilian Cities Are in Danger
of Becoming News Deserts,
According to New Survey," Knight
Center for Journalism in the
Americas, November 28, 2018.

70   **another government
initiative:** Júlio Lubianco,
"Bolsonaro Removes Obligation of
Government Agencies to Publish
Public Notices in Brazilian Print
Newspapers," Knight Center
for Journalism in the Americas,
September 11, 2019.

70   **Janz's words:** Amanda Meade,
"Fairfax journalists Condemn
Proposed $30m Job Cuts and
Political Positioning," *Guardian*,
April 6, 2017.

71   **I was fascinated:** Alex
Dixon, "More Loss of Local News:
Questions with April Lindgren,"
University of North Carolina
Hussman School of Journalism and
Media, December 5, 2018.

104   CHAPTER FIVE

73   **Trust was low:** "State of Public Trust in Local News," Gallup and the Knight Foundation, October 29, 2019.

74   **The first step:** Elizabeth Green, "Why I'm Placing My Bets on the American Journalism Project," Medium, February 25, 2019.

75   **became a dominant player:** Justin Ellis, "What Makes the Texas Tribune's Event Business So Successful?" Nieman Lab, September 27, 2013.

76   **Two revenue paths:** Heidi Legg, "A Landscape Study of Local News Models Across America," Harvard Kennedy School Shorenstein Center, July 3, 2019.

78   **so infuriated the populace:** Margaret Sullivan, "How One Small News Organization's Investigative Reporting Took Down Puerto Rico's Governor," *Washington Post*, July 27, 2019.

80   **full-time statehouse reporters:** Katerina Eva Matsa and Jan Lauren Boyles, "America's Shifting Statehouse Press," Pew Research Center: Journalism & Media, July 10, 2014.

80   **"the Billionaire Local Newspaper Club":** Heidi Legg, "A Landscape Study of Local News Models Across America."

81   **James Wright:** Wesley Pippert and Nadine Epstein, "Can Sheldon Adelson Turn Nevada Red?" Slate, July 30, 2017.

82   **"mobilizers" and "accelerators":** Heidi Legg, "A Landscape Study of Local News Models Across America."

83   **the Community Network:** Mathew Ingram, "Facebook Is Both Killing and Funding Local Journalism," *Columbia Journalism Review,* July 18, 2019.

84   **David Chavern:** Margaret Sullivan, "Facebook Launches a Charm Offensive—and Vows to Pay (Some) News Organizations for Their Journalism," *Washington Post,* October 25, 2019.

84   **News Media Alliance:** "News Media Alliance Applauds Senators Kennedy and Klobuchar for Introducing Journalism Competition & Preservation Act," News Media Alliance, June 3, 2019.

84   **Nicholas Lemann:** Nicholas Lemann, "Can Journalism Be Saved?" *New York Review of Books*, February 27, 2020.

CONCLUSION

89   **Clay Shirky:** Clay Shirky, "Newspapers and Thinking the Unthinkable," *New York Times*, March 13, 2009.

90   **the haves and the have-nots:** Keach Hagey, Lukas Alpert, and Yaryna Serkez, "In News Industry, a Stark Divide Between Haves and Have-Nots," *Wall Street Journal*, May 4, 2019.

90   **doggedly told the unsavory story:** Tiffany Hsu, "The Jeffrey Epstein Case Was Cold, Until a Miami Herald Reporter Got Accusers to Talk," *New York Times*, July 9, 2019.

91   **Joshua Benton of Nieman Lab:** https://twitter.com/jbenton/status/1153367813291225088.

91   **Two researchers at Duke University:** Philip Napoli and Jessica Mahone, "Local Newspapers Are Suffering, but They're Still (by Far) the Most Significant Journalism Producers in Their Communities," Nieman Lab, September 9, 2019.

93   **The column hit a nerve:** Margaret Sullivan, "Too Little for So Many, Even in the *Times*," *New York Times*, June 1, 2013.

93   **in a 2018 talk:** "How to Restore Trust in the Media: Abernathy's Testimony to the Knight Commission," UNC Hussman School of Journalism and Media, April 27, 2018.

94   **Gallup/Knight poll:** "State of Public Trust in Local News," Gallup and the Knight Foundation.

Columbia Global Reports is a publishing imprint from Columbia University that commissions authors to do original on-site reporting around the globe on a wide range of issues. The resulting novella-length books offer new ways to look at and understand the world that can be read in a few hours. Most readers are curious and busy. Our books are for them.

Subscribe to Columbia Global Reports and get six books a year in the mail in advance of publication. globalreports.columbia.edu/subscribe

New Kings of the World: Dispatches from Bollywood, Dizi, and K-Pop
Fatima Bhutto

State of War: MS-13 and El Salvador's World of Violence
William Wheeler

Vigil: Hong Kong on the Brink
Jeffrey Wasserstrom

The Call: Inside the Global Saudi Religious Project
Krithika Varagur

The Socialist Awakening: What's Different Now About the Left
John B. Judis

Carte Blanche: The Erosion of Medical Consent
Harriet A. Washington